Forest School

IN PRACTICE

SAGE was founded in 1965 by Sara Miller McCune to support the dissemination of usable knowledge by publishing innovative and high-quality research and teaching content. Today, we publish over 900 journals, including those of more than 400 learned societies, more than 800 new books per year, and a growing range of library products including archives, data, case studies, reports, and video. SAGE remains majority-owned by our founder, and after Sara's lifetime will become owned by a charitable trust that secures our continued independence.

Los Angeles | London | New Delhi | Singapore | Washington DC | Melbourne

Forest School
IN PRACTICE

Sara Knight

Los Angeles | London | New Delhi
Singapore | Washington DC | Melbourne

Los Angeles | London | New Delhi
Singapore | Washington DC | Melbourne

SAGE Publications Ltd
1 Oliver's Yard
55 City Road
London EC1Y 1SP

SAGE Publications Inc.
2455 Teller Road
Thousand Oaks, California 91320

SAGE Publications India Pvt Ltd
B 1/I 1 Mohan Cooperative Industrial Area
Mathura Road
New Delhi 110 044

SAGE Publications Asia-Pacific Pte Ltd
3 Church Street
#10-04 Samsung Hub
Singapore 049483

Editor: Jude Bowen
Assistant editor: George Knowles
Production editor: Nicola Marshall
Copyeditor: Sharon Cawood
Proofreader: Roza I.M. El-Eini
Indexer: David Rudeforth
Marketing manager: Dilhara Attygalle
Cover design: Wendy Scott
Typeset by: C&M Digitals (P) Ltd, Chennai, India
Printed and bound in Great Britain by Bell and
Bain Ltd, Glasgow

Library of Congress Control Number: 2016953340

British Library Cataloguing in Publication data

A catalogue record for this book is available from the British
Library

ISBN 978-1-4739-4891-4
ISBN 978-1-4739-4892-1 (pbk)

At SAGE we take sustainability seriously. Most of our products are printed in the UK using FSC papers and boards.
When we print overseas we ensure sustainable papers are used as measured by the PREPS grading system.
We undertake an annual audit to monitor our sustainability.

To the memory of my dear husband David, still beside me every day

Contents

About the Author

 **Sara Knight** is a teacher and Forest School leader. She contributes to the development of Forest School in the UK, publishing academic papers and books on the subject, and is a keynote speaker at conferences worldwide. Since retiring as a university lecturer, she continues to play in the woods and write about it.

Acknowledgement

Grateful thanks to all my fellow members in the Forest School Association who have contributed, suggested and played with ideas for this book.

Introduction

Forest School has been delivered in the UK for over twenty years, spreading inexorably since the mid-1990s. The history of the movement is recorded variously elsewhere, and is most readily accessible on the website of the Forest School Association (Cree & McCree, 2014). Over that time, not only has its delivery coverage spread but its influence has spread even further. By 2015, the Forest School Association (FSA) had over 1200 members, and it was estimated by then that over 1200 people had completed Forest School leadership training at Level 3. In this book, I argue that Forest School exemplifies ways of being in and with nature that are essential for the health of the individual, society and the planet. I will also argue that the 'Forest' element is important, illustrating the special relationship between humans and trees. Forest School is also spreading across the globe, with Forest School, Forest Kindergarten and similar associations springing up across Europe, Asia, Canada and Australasia, although that is largely outside the scope of this book. My concern is with the UK, where the strains of modern life are having deleterious effects on the health and well-being of many people. Forest School for all is not the only answer but it does offer benefits that all can access, which does increase its value.

As an active member of the FSA, I was gaining the impression by 2015 that the expansion of Forest School provision was still continuing despite the cuts in government funding to the education, health and social sectors. To find out the range and depth of Forest School activity, a questionnaire was circulated to the 220 attendees of the 2015 FSA conference and 59 responses were collated – a response rate of 28 per cent. This shows that attendees who responded came from across the UK (Figure 0.1). There was also a small group of attendees from Scotland, but they did not complete questionnaires, and three from Forest School Canada. The home nations and some English regions have strong local groups and most send representation to the national conference once a year.

The survey also showed how diverse the groups have become that are participating in Forest School sessions. Figure 0.2 shows the groups that practitioners are working with. The largest group participating in Forest School still appears to be the preschool sector, where the roots

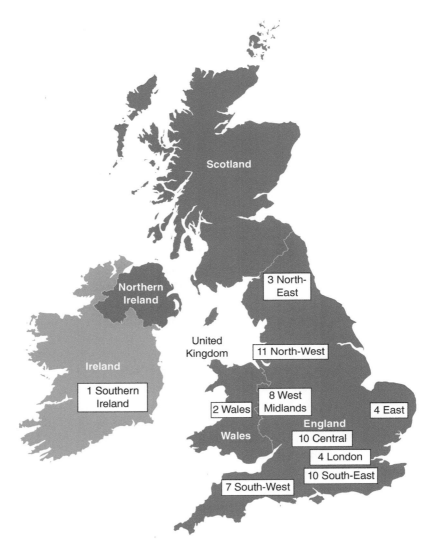

FIGURE 0.1   Location Map

of Forest School lie. However, closer analysis shows that if one adds the column for primary schools where children aged 4–11 years are all participating to the column for infants, who are children aged 4–7 years, it is clear that it is the 4–7-year-olds who make up the largest group participating in Forest School sessions. In addition, further analysis of the preschool group shows that almost all of these are groups of 3–5-year-olds, making the 4- and 5-year-olds the children most likely to participate in Forest School sessions in the UK. The variations in the curricular and school systems across the home nations makes this a slightly confusing picture, so, in Part 2, we will consider these differences and how this impacts on children's experiences of Forest School.

With younger children, the influence of Forest School and similar initiatives has encouraged an upsurge in messier outdoor provision, with mud kitchens and growing areas in most daycare settings, so that children are engaging with their natural environments in sensory ways, but few under-3s are taken into wild spaces beyond their settings. Part 1 will discuss settings where wilder outdoor provision does exist for younger children and how it is managed. The dearth of Forest School provision for the under-3s may in part account for the other growth area seen in Figure 0.2, of family groups, most frequently described on the questionnaires as parent and toddler groups, but also recorded are whole-family sessions through the longer school holidays. Add these figures to the community groups, which are recorded as Forest School open to a whole community, and the figures are even more impressive. There is also a growing number of holiday and after-school Forest School, catering for the most part for children who have had a Forest School experience earlier in their school careers and wish to

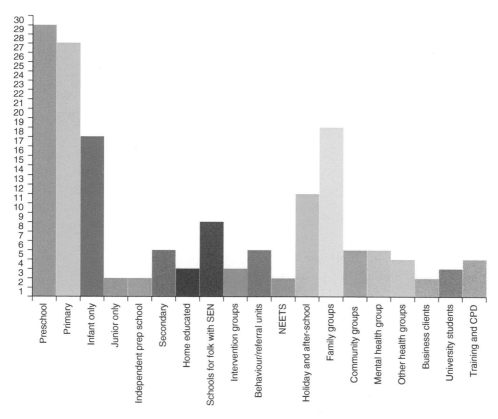

FIGURE 0.2   Graph of Ages and Types

continue when the schools are no longer providing it. This would seem to represent a grass-roots recognition of wilder experiences that we will explore in Chapter 14.

Another significant group is those for whom Forest School is an alternative educational provision to replace or supplement mainstream education. Schools for people with learning difficulties were early to recognise the benefits of outdoor learning, and Forest School is a pedagogy that is in harmony with the pedagogies used in what are often termed special schools. Chapter 10 will consider this area. The emphasis on developing the emotional intelligence of participants has led to the adoption of Forest School by units and schools supporting pupils with behavioural issues or who are disaffected from education and society. Chapter 12 will discuss these areas of Forest School provision. Chapter 11 will also discuss occurrences of using Forest School to support other vulnerable groups in mainstream settings. Dorling (2016) criticises the treatment of vulnerable secondary school pupils in the English education system; Part 4 seeks to explore how Forest School is being used to support them.

Recently, members of the FSA have noted increasing numbers of practitioners working with adults to support their health needs. Most frequently, they are working with people with mental health issues, but practitioners are also working with recovering drug addicts and those convalescing from other serious conditions. The emphasis in Forest School training on being client-led and on taking time to be mindful of the environment creates a healing atmosphere in Forest School sessions, as will be considered in Chapter 13.

Of the 59 surveyed practitioners, all were either qualified to Level 3 or were in training at Level 3. This is the Forest School leadership award that enables practitioners to manage Forest School sessions. The training is extensive, typically taking a year to complete, and covers a wide range of topics, including theories of brain development and some bushcraft skills. To preserve the quality of Forest School delivery, it is important that practitioners are all trained to these standards, and by training organisations of quality. The FSA works closely with the GB Forest School Trainers' Network, as can be seen on their website (FSA, 2015a), and is working towards an endorsement scheme for trainers.

All practitioners bring their own experiences to the training, which are equally diverse, from teachers to wildlife rangers and beyond. This diversity ensures that the Forest School movement is lively, creative and evolving. It also means that continuing professional development (CPD) is essential, particularly if practitioners wish to offer sessions to a range of different groups. This point is made in several places in the book and ideas are included in each chapter for practitioners to try out. All of the surveyed practitioners were actively engaged in CPD, including the workshops available at the conference.

This book seeks to explore the diversity of groups now participating in Forest School across the UK in five parts.

PART 1: NATURE PROVISION FOR VERY YOUNG CHILDREN

The UK has always had a few day nurseries led by practitioners interested in engaging their children with the natural world, and a few pioneers championing the importance of this strategy. The McMillan sisters and Susan Isaacs promoted outdoor space, Elinor Goldschmied and Maria Montessori encouraged the use of natural materials, but the spread of the Forest School ethos over the last 20 years has helped to focus the policies of increasing numbers of settings on embracing the importance of outdoor spaces for our youngest children. In this part, we look at some examples of how the needs of our youngest children are being met, and reflect on the implications of the challenges they have overcome.

PART 2: FOREST SCHOOL OPPORTUNITIES FOR 3—5-YEAR-OLDS

Over the last 20 years, Forest School in the UK has become most readily available for children in this age range, with more settings training staff and developing access to wild spaces. The progress they have made has been shaped and supported differently across the home nations, and this section aims to explore what has happened and why this might be the case. The role of the Forestry Commission, and that of the devolved parliaments, has been important. So, too, has been the location of key individuals who have driven the agenda along on their home turf. The development of the Forest School Association from a special interest group to independence, the influence of the Trainers' Network, and the individuality of the national curricula in each country will all be considered through the lens of provision for this age group.

PART 3: FOREST SCHOOL AT PRIMARY SCHOOL

Research evidence is building about the impact Forest School experiences have on children in the primary school age range, which for the purposes of this part will be confined to 6–11 years old. From stimulating writing to improving teamwork, the results are impressive. It is interesting, therefore, to consider what the stimuli are that spur schools on to include Forest School in their offer, and whether these are primarily driven by curriculum needs or by personal, social, health and economic education (PSHE). Forest School is also being adopted in the independent sector and parallels are drawn with Steiner pedagogy.

PART 4: FOREST SCHOOL AT SECONDARY SCHOOL

The older the child, the less likely they are to be offered a Forest School experience. By the time children reach the age of 12, they are usually only offered Forest School if they have an additional need that cannot be met by conventional schooling. It could be argued that we all have these additional needs at some point in our lives. Perhaps by looking at the dividends that accrue to those groups who are offered these opportunities, it is possible to deduce the likely benefits to the whole secondary generation if Forest School were to be a universal entitlement.

PART 5: OTHER FOREST SCHOOL OCCURRENCES

As the benefits of Forest School become more widely known, practitioners are exploring how the principles can help others who are failing to thrive in modern society. With increases in obesity, alcohol abuse and work-related illnesses, it could be said that modern society is not the healthiest environment for many of us. By looking at the creative uses of Forest School with families and with different groups of adults, we may conclude that there are Forest School lessons that we can all learn.

SUGGESTED FURTHER RESEARCH

- There are many sections of the Forest School Association website available to non-members: see www.forestschoolassociation.org/
- Explore the range of outdoor activities available to children and adults via the following two websites:
  - Council for Learning Outside the Classroom: www.lotc.org.uk/
  - Institute for Outdoor Learning: www.outdoor-learning.org/

- Consider Forest School and similar initiatives outside the UK that are influenced by or participated in by FSA members, for example:
    - Bush Schools in Australia: http://preciouschildhood.blogspot.co.uk/2012/05/bush-school-nature-education-in.html
    - Forest School Canada: www.forestschoolcanada.ca/
    - The European Institute for Outdoor Adventure Education and Experiential Learning: www.eoe-network.eu/home/

Part 1

Nature Provision for Very Young Children

1

Nature Kindergarten

This chapter explores settings where young children, some as young as 2 years old, spend most of their time at daycare outside. Two case studies are considered, and points for discussion are raised. The reasons why it is important for young children to spend time outside will begin to be unpicked, a thread of thought that runs through this section of three chapters.

Across the UK, there are just a few settings that are aiming to provide everyday outdoor care and education for the very young, but they are increasing in number. Initial attempts to set these up were made challenging by the registration agencies, who found their own knowledge being extended by this new concept. The two case studies represent successes in Scotland and England, and point the way for others to follow.

CASE STUDY 1.1: AUCHLONE NATURE KINDERGARTEN

In 2006, Claire Warden opened the Auchlone Nature Kindergarten, a daycare setting in woodland eight miles from Perth, Scotland. It caters for children from the age of 2 upwards. This includes out-of-school provision for school-aged children which stretches to week-long camps in the summer for 5- and 6-year-olds, with older children as youth leaders. Claire's company, Mindstretchers (www.mindstretchers.co.uk/), is well known across the Forest School community as a supplier of quality

(Continued)

(Continued)

equipment and helpful literature, and Claire herself is an academic as well as a practitioner, involved in research and lecturing across the world, so Auchlone Nature Kindergarten is operated by a team of trusted nursery staff.

Their curriculum is nature based, following the Scottish 'Pre Birth to Three' for children aged 2–3 years and the Scottish 'Curriculum for Excellence' (CfE) for children from 3 to 18 years. For the 2–5-year-olds, they use Claire's recording system of PLODS (Possible Lines of Development). Children's voices and the process of learning are recorded in Talking and Thinking Floorbooks™, a method developed by Claire Warden. These books are created with the children; they share their ideas and contribute their understanding at their own level. They document group learning experiences and consultations and value each child as an individual, recording their progress and understanding throughout. These and staff's Post-it notes enable the staff to keep a book for each child's individual learning stories. They record the child's interactions with an event in the kindergarten – one they may have initiated or been invited to join. Staff then reflect on these interactions and how they relate to the Scottish curricula. From those reflections come the PLODS (see Figure 1.1), which then inform how staff plan for activities in subsequent days.

The children at Auchlone are outside in all weathers and all seasons but there are two indoor spaces that they can use. One is a small gatehouse to the estate where the wood is situated. This has interlinking small rooms with cabinets to store nature's treasures such as stones, bones and feathers. They are grouped elegantly in ways

Making Soup
October 2013

Birth to Three: 1,2,3,4.

Sophie's Theories:

- Soup needs different ingredients and needs to be stirred.
- Cooking with a friend is better than on your own.
- Mud is Fun!!!

Possible Lines of Development for Sophie:

- Provide Sophie with opportunities to make real soup.
- Provide Sophie with opportunities to look at receipes and choose some
- Investigate with Sophie other uses for mud.

FIGURE 1.1   PLODS – Possible Lines of Development

FIGURE 1.2   The Mud Kitchen

(Continued)

reminiscent of Montessori materials, and children can handle them and reflect on their place in the natural order. The other, adjacent, building is a more open wooden structure of two halves. One side has a wood burner surrounded by seating areas covered in blankets, and the other a kitchen area for food preparation with and for the children. Natural mobiles and displays decorate the space which feels like something between a tipi and a Scandinavian cottage.

These buildings are at the bottom of the slope up to the main woods, as is a mud kitchen (Figure 1.2), a fire pit and a cultivated growing area for food for the children. Again, they are involved in the growing process. Nowhere are the children restricted from participation in the running of their space. Areas merge into each other with a sense of the flow of experiential learning. Winding paths lead up into extensive woodland. Just off the paths are fallen trees to climb on, evidence of den-making activity, fire pits and a range of structures for purposes known to their creators if not to a casual visitor. In one clearing, one can see a lake – the local inspectors have required this to be fenced off from unsupervised approaches: the only restriction that can be seen on following a nature pedagogy.

CASE STUDY 1.2: FOREST KINDERGARTEN SEVENOAKS

In 2014, Caroline Watts opened her Forest Kindergarten near Sevenoaks in Kent (www. forest-kindergarten.co.uk). It is a testament to her dedication that, after surmounting many difficulties with registration as a daycare setting, she was subsequently awarded an 'Outstanding' grade from a 2014 Ofsted inspection, praising its 'child-led, vibrant environment' and the positive impact it has on children's learning, and noting that the nursery 'is unique in that it uses the natural environment to maintain this'.

The National Trust has provided the wood for the nursery, and it undertakes the necessary safety inspections of the site, which has no indoor space for the children at all. The only shelter available is a large tent (see Figure 1.3), which contains books and blankets where a comfortable and cosy quiet space can be created. There is a composting toilet on-site. The kindergarten is sessional, running from 9 am to 2 pm on three days of the week and 9 am to 12 noon on two days, and can take 14 children per session. The children are between 3 and 5 years old, and attend a minimum of two sessions a week. Parents are given clear advice as to the clothing the children will need. During the school holidays, Caroline takes older children, up to 7 years old.

The sessions will always include breaks taken around the fire where warm drinks and food can be prepared. As well as the small wood which is the hub of the kindergarten, the site is surrounded by fields, and a green lane leads off into the countryside on the opposite side of the access lane to the wood. The children frequently set off along here to lead the adults into exploratory adventures that add additional layers of inventiveness to the adventures to be had through tool use and tree climbing around the base camp.

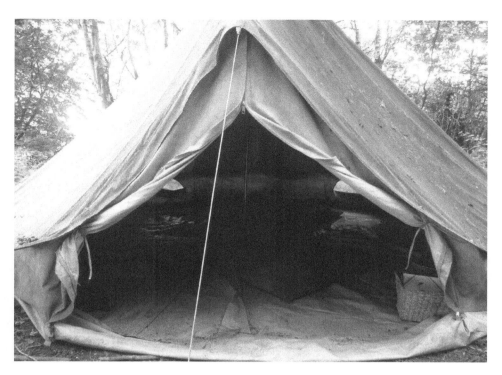

FIGURE 1.3   The Only Shelter

The kindergarten follows the English Statutory Framework for Early Years. Records are mainly kept photographically or digitally and are available to parents as well as satisfying the government requirements. The activities routinely include imaginative and creative opportunities, and cooking opportunities. Nature exploration and connection to nature through digging, collecting and observing the changing seasons are central (see Figure 1.4). Construction tools are available, which encourage finding opportunities for mathematics, and understanding of the world through natural materials.

Physical development is supported when exploring the woodland, tree climbing, trying out rope swings, den building and making seesaws. Around the campfire, there are opportunities for circle time and daily reflection time as well as music games, dance, singing and rhymes.

It is interesting to note that neither of the case study settings takes children younger than 2 years old, and, although Case Study 1.1 does take 2-year-olds, they are for the most part children who are in the latter half of that year of growth. Being outside for the majority of the day is clearly a challenge for children 2 years old and younger. This is partly due to the ratio between surface and core in the body. Very young children have much higher skin to body mass ratios, making them more vulnerable to extremes of temperature.

FIGURE 1.4 Exploring the Treeness of Tree

This is not to say that babies and toddlers do not benefit from spending prolonged periods of time outside. Up until the 1950s in the UK it was commonplace to place babies in prams outside to gain the benefits of breathing fresh air, and toddlers accompanied older children and adults as they worked in gardens and fields. But, from the Industrial Revolution onwards, this declined, particularly amongst those poor who moved into cramped and crowded accommodation in the expanding urban areas around new factories. The discovery of the parlous state of health of the urban poor in the 1870s led to the founding of the McMillan sisters' outdoor nursery in Deptford (Cunningham, 2006: 184) as it was realised that to deprive very young children of fresh air and outdoor exercise appeared to stunt their growth. However, since the 1950s, the increased need for parents to both work outside the home has led to a corresponding increase in daycare settings, not all of which were initially equipped to provide a rich outdoor environment for their charges.

There are many reasons why free access to rich outdoor provision is important for all children. This chapter will only explore a few of them and it will take all the chapters of this section to build a full picture of why this is so important, and how it relates to Forest School practice.

The most obvious reasons for providing regular and protracted outdoor learning opportunities are the physical ones. The Victorians found that the urban poor, living in cramped and enclosed conditions, were smaller and less healthy than their equally poor country cousins, hence the foundation of the Deptford Day Nursery by the McMillan sisters. Increased opportunities for fresh air and for vigorous outdoor exercise stimulate increases in bone and muscle development. In the two case studies, children are free to walk up and down hills across different natural surfaces. They can climb trees and logs, and build dens from wood and brush. They dodge under, round and through a range of natural barriers. This is *We're Going on a Lion Hunt* (Cuyler & Mathieu, 2014) in a real way.

More physical reasons to establish habits of going outside include the rise across the wealthier nations of childhood obesity. Figures from the Health Survey for England (HSE) for 2013 revealed that among children aged 2–15, 16 per cent of boys and 15 per cent of girls were classed as obese, and 14 per cent of both boys and girls were classed as overweight. Overall, 30 per cent of boys and 29 per cent of girls were classed as either overweight or obese (Boodhna, 2013). Undoubtedly, this is a major national concern as an obese child is at double the risk of becoming an overweight or obese adult. Obesity is linked to a poor diet but the link between obesity and levels of exercise is stronger. Across the Western world, health experts (for example, Berntsen et al., 2010; Jouret et al., 2007) are concluding that watching TV increases obesity, exercise decreases it, and establishing habits of exercise in preschool children is key to long-term success.

Establishing habits of exercise and being in the fresh air are achieved by *being* active and *being* outside on a regular basis, as in our case studies. As I have stated before (Knight, 2013: 19), neural pathways are established in the brain in response to activity and the myelinisation of those pathways – the process that makes that activity a part of the child's way of being – occurs in response to repetitions of that activity. Being outside regularly and being free to stretch and grow makes a child *want* to be outside regularly and be free to stretch and grow. It is much easier to create these healthy ways of being while the brain is young and plastic. Once myelinisation has occurred, it then becomes harder to change the neural pathway, so that the older we are, the harder it becomes to change our habits. You can teach an old dog new tricks but it takes longer and takes more dedication. It is easier, healthier and happier to do it while children are very young.

We can hardwire children to be healthier and fitter by enabling them to spend more time outside being active. However, we do need to be aware of other hardwiring that is going on. Observe an 18-month-old with a computer tablet or a smart phone. You will soon see them stroke the screen to change the display. In our fast-moving world, each generation is biologically different from the previous one by virtue of the wiring that their environment has stimulated in their brains. It is this ability for our large brains to adapt and change that has made the human race so successful. Unfortunately, our bodies do not evolve as quickly. The human eye does not fully develop in most children until they are 7 or 8 years old, which is why children younger than this find it hard to judge the speed and distance of cars when learning to cross roads safely. Their eyes, and the bits of brain that interpret the visual messages, are developing both with age and in response to their experiences. Concerns are beginning to be expressed that too much screen time for anyone is a problem (The Vision Council, 2015), and some are suggesting that the next generation will not have the same ability to see at a distance just because they have not spent long enough as a child looking into the distance – something called 'computer vision syndrome' in the USA. It is only possible to look into the distance when you are outside and can see across a landscape, or are looking through a window at that landscape. This is not to advise wholesale rejection of new technology – apps to identify natural objects from ladybirds to constellations can be both useful and educational. But, as so often in life, moderation and consideration of outcomes need to be minded.

In summary, young children need to spend regular and prolonged periods of time outside in natural surroundings in order to be healthy, to develop fully and to establish habits that will keep them healthy as adults. These are just the reasons for creating the best healthy human machines from the raw material we are born with and giving them the best chance of staying healthy. However, we are already faced with difficulties in achieving these outcomes. Whilst children are happy to be outside in all weathers, many adults are not. A feature of both case studies is the dedication of the adults to creating these amazing places. As Claire Warden has said:

> The most important aspect of learning with nature is the adult views on what nature offers children, and whether the practitioners and parents are motivated by nature themselves. In some environments, the adults have no residual memory of making mud pies, petal perfume, or a den. If a team does not have an 'inner glow,' what will they draw on when the rain comes down or the challenge of delivery of curriculum seems to be more important than being outside? (Warden, 2015)

As in Auchlone, Caroline Watts from the Forest Kindergarten Sevenoaks (Case Study 1.2) has created her environment from her love and passion for nature, and is supported by staff who are equally passionate about nature and about children. Between them, her team has a shared knowledge of early years care and education, of bushcraft and of outdoor cookery and crafts. They don't all know all of these things; an aspiring manager in any business or industry does not expect to know it all themselves but they 'know a man who does' – in other words, they will pull a team together that has the requisite skill set. Some of those skills will have been rooted in childhood experiences, the memories Claire cites that have inspired them to offer the same or similar experiences to the next generation. Unfortunately, there seems to be at least one generation, possibly two, in the UK, where the majority of people did not have those rich outdoor experiences as children.

Bird (2007) identified how the 'right to roam' in childhood has declined in four generations, and the subsequent effects on children's participation in their natural surroundings. The children he observed typically spent their leisure time indoors, in their gardens or at clubs and leisure venues. These are the children who will now be training to work in our daycare settings, and without explicit experiential education it will be hard to ensure that the children they care for will have the outdoor experiences they need. In the graph in the Introduction (Figure 0.2), it can be seen that training in Forest School is starting to become a part of some undergraduate programmes. For the most part, this is found in training programmes for early years educators, but often the modules are optional, and so the spread of experiential knowledge is to a self-selecting group of students. We will return to this issue in Part 2.

GOING FORWARD

REFLECTIONS ON FOREST SCHOOL

This chapter has emphasised the importance of regular and long-term access to the outdoors, the first principle of Forest School Association (Knight, 2016b). Reflect on what 'long term' means to you. If Auchlone is a Nature Kindergarten and Sevenoaks is a Forest Kindergarten, is there a difference in what happens there? In both settings, children can reflect on their activities around a fire. Is this Forest School? Consider the websites of each setting and reflect on their offering:

www.forest-kindergarten.co.uk/index.php

www.mindstretchers.co.uk/Auchlone%20Nature%20Kindergarten.cfm

IDEAS FOR PRACTICE: SMELL POTS

In the quote from Claire above, she spoke about making petal perfume. This is something most children will love to do. Encourage children to focus on their sense of smell by collecting natural objects in a pot, crushing them and sniffing the result. They can:

- test each other and see if they can guess what it is
- make their own perfumes by selecting their favourite flower petals and water. Again, this needs crushing to release the smell; this only smells pleasant for about 12 hours, unless you are going to heat the pots over the fire and distil the flower essence, when you can have a meaningful discussion about decay and consign the remains to the composting area
- use their smell pots to 'illustrate' a story – 'we walked past the *fir tree* and then the *blackberry bush* before we got to the *grass* by the *stream*' – four pots, each representing one sensory experience.

They will have more ideas, too. Enabling them to experiment could set their feet on the path to a love of science.

FURTHER READING

- A simple web search using the key words 'natural, health, UK' will link to services across the UK using nature to promote health, in adults as well as children. The

Natural Health Service on Merseyside at www.naturalhealthservice.org.uk/ links to a fact sheet about Forest School in the area. You will also find a link to a briefing paper from the Faculty of Public Health and Natural England – www.fph.org.uk/uploads/bs_great_outdoors.pdf – and other useful sites.

- Two papers on obesity have been cited (Berntsen et al., 2010; Jouret et al., 2007), and there are many more from across the developed world to read.
- A report to look at is on the changing relationship between children and nature, a report for Natural England entitled 'Childhood and Nature: A Survey on Changing Relationships with Nature across Generations' (Hilary, 2009), available via the Natural England website at http://publications.naturalengland.org.uk/publication/853658314964992

2

Urban Forest School

When is a wood not a wood? This chapter deals with Forest School in urban areas where woods may be in short supply. So, what are the solutions? A lady from Iceland once asked: 'How can I do Forest School when our trees grow no higher than my knee?' It is about taking advantage of what you have – in Australia, they often call what they do 'Bush School', as they have access to bush rather than woods. But for Forest School, trees are important, speaking to us as they do from our cultural and spiritual heritage. Forest School Principle 2 refers to sessions that take place in a woodland or natural wooded environment to support the development of a relationship between the learner and the natural world (FSA, 2011). The case studies in this chapter are of practitioners based in the centre of cities, one in London and one in Bristol, who have all found their own answers. In inner cities, the number of trees that a group can access may be limited; Milchem (2011: 21) records a group using the grounds of a large house in South London. Fortunately, the smaller you are, the bigger and more numerous the trees look. And the fewer trees that you come across in your normal life, the more important it becomes to create opportunities to encounter them 'up close and personal'. This chapter starts with some of the reasons why this is the case before suggesting some ways to create the opportunities. And, on the way, there is a discussion of another important issue, that of men in childcare.

CASE STUDY 2.1: FREE RANGE URBAN KIDS, MILLFIELDS PARK, HACKNEY

Hackney is an East London borough with a very varied demographic and housing, and around 15,000 families with children under the age of 5. Fortunately, it has some rich green spaces and parks, including the Hackney Marshes, the Lee Valley, Wick Woodland and Millfields Park. Free Range Urban Kids began in November 2014 by running 2-hour sessions for 2–5-year-olds three days a week and, having achieved Ofsted registration, now run full days (since January 2016) as a completely outdoor nursery. Hayley Mitchell and her co-founder, Elizabeth Hassay, are both mothers, one of Danish and one of German descent. Both are familiar with education in the outdoors, and Hayley has now trained as a Forest School leader. On a piece of council-owned property, the site is surrounded by fencing with one gate for access, creating a safe space in an urban environment. There are no on-site storage facilities, so everything needed for the sessions is transported in bike trailers. Certain temporary structures, such as a wormery, a bug hotel and the log circle, can be left.

A sign saying 'Forest School Sessions in progress' ensures that, although open to the public at all times, it is largely avoided by the local users of the rest of the park while sessions take place. Whilst the largest area of the site is a grassland, the second has a section of wood with a range of oak, ash, maple, elder and silver birch, and a row of conifers providing sound protection from the nearby busy Chatsworth Road. A third area is predominantly made up of rose bushes and elders which create the perfect climbing and den-making area. Tarpaulins strung between trees cover areas where children can play musical instruments, make natural art with mud and leaves, or participate in snack and story time. The council does not permit fires within the park as a general rule but it has given the group special permission to do so after it was explained that it was an integral part of the Forest School ethos.

During its first year, children came to climb, dig, run, observe, make, build and connect with nature. Parents recorded how the space provided allows more freedom and how this has had a positive impact on their children's behaviour. Just 3500 square metres have enabled children to observe the full range of seasonal changes and to connect with their natural surroundings in a way previously unavailable without travelling out of the city. Currently, Free Range operates as a private forest kindergarten, but it would love to find funding for low-income families and aims to open a not-for-profit branch of the business in order to do so, recognising that inclusivity is central to Forest School's principles.

There are planned activities for every session which link to the season and environment. However, there is a child-led, open-ended structure that facilitates choice and autonomy, so the activities are there as a safety net for those children who need inspiration. This provides a level playing field and equal opportunities for everyone, allowing development at all levels with the chance to collaborate and create. Numeracy and literacy can be developed in this way, through observation, communication and construction. The observations made already are that these children are confident, happy, articulate and have a good sense of themselves and the world around them. Hayley explains: 'The children can run about and they learn in a holistic way, about how the wind feels, what trees and grass smell like, what they feel like, and the "toys" are what they find and what they want them to be, so a stick can be a wand, for example, and there are plenty of sticks.'

Base camp features a tarpaulin over the trees to provide cover from the elements and two pop-up tents (one a cosy area and the other housing a potty). Hayley added: 'We cram in work when our little ones sleep, holding meetings and interviews in the park. We have completed paediatric and outdoor first aid courses; hired wonderful Forest School practitioners, and gathered together Forest School equipment.'

CASE STUDY 2.2: A LETTER FROM GREENBANK FOREST SCHOOL CHILDMINDING

We are childminders and trained Forest School leaders and have been running as a predominantly outdoor-based Forest School setting since September 2014. We are home-based in Easton, an inner-city neighbourhood in East Bristol. We have 11 children on roll, most of whom are with us two or three days a week from 8.30 until either 5pm or 6 pm. We look after 6 children each day, ranging between 10 months and 4 years old.

For the first 9 months, we used a small local inner-city nature reserve. Unfortunately, it became evident that it was being over-used by dog walkers and locals using the site in the evening, often leaving broken glass and drug litter. So, we decided to invest in a 9-seater van and move our Forest School activities to Leigh Woods. This is a large ancient woodland at the edge of the city, a 20-minute drive from our house.

The children are dropped off at our house at 8.30 am. Around 9.30, we drive off to Leigh Woods, arriving there for 10 am. During term time we leave the woods around 2.45 to enable us to do the school pick-up. In school holidays we tend to stay out longer. On average, we spend 3 or 4 days a week in Leigh Woods and the other days roaming round other outdoor spaces, including National Trust Parks and woodlands.

On arrival in the woods, we put the kids in wellies and waterproofs, which we provide. What happens next is child led. If the children have already said they want to play with water, we'll walk to the stream. If they have requested a fire, we'll make our way to an appropriate space. Often the children want to continue a play narrative they started at a previous session so we return to the same spot. Sometimes we just go for a long walk and explore the woods.

Because our age group runs from babies to preschool we have to accommodate sleeps, which tend to be in carriers on our backs, in the buggy or in a hammock. Given that we do not have access to indoor space in the woods, during the winter months we provide gloves, hats and extra fleeces for the children. The youngest that

(Continued)

(Continued)

are unable to run around to keep warm need particular attention and are often carried in a carrier to share body heat. Despite this, during the coldest days in winter, we reduce our outdoor time down to two hours.

We often bring in resources, for instance: a portable fire pit, knives, rope, a rope swing, hammocks, a rope ladder, mud kitchen equipment, bug pots, etc. These are freely available to the children. We also always have story books, which can lead to a follow-on activity if that is where the mood takes us.

Whilst the sessions vary greatly, we always bring snacks and a packed lunch, sometimes supplemented by something cooked on the fire. This provides some structure to the sessions and provides a good opportunity to sit down together for moments of reflection. The children now know to build their own base camp by finding logs and moving them into a circle or square. On wet days, we put up a large tarp to keep dry during lunch.

We absolutely love Forest School. We have seen our mindees' self-esteem and resilience come on in leaps and bounds. It is amazing to see how the boy who was very reluctant to leave the safety of the buggy in his first weeks in the woods is now the first to jump in the muddy puddle, climb up the steep hill or grab that stick to battle a dragon.

Mike Williams and Charissa de Zeeuw (www.greenbankforestschoolchildminding.co.uk)

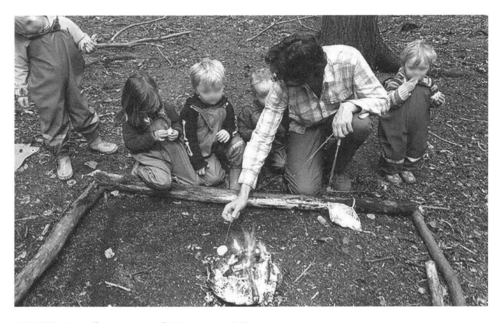

FIGURE 2.1   Greenbank Childminder Mike

As noted in Chapter 1, many parents have themselves missed having a childhood rich in outdoor opportunities, and because of this they are less likely to provide such opportunities for their very young children, at a time when the brain is being wired for life. Milchem (2011: 17) records the effect of this deprivation on one such child, a child of 4 years old who was afraid to walk on the grass in a park because he had never walked on an uneven surface before. He did not know if this uneven surface was safe, nor how to adjust his balance to cope with it. This is not the effect of a deliberate lack of care, merely the combined effects of living in urban surroundings and parents not perceiving that access to nature is important at a young age. Immediately, one can see some of the long-term implications for this child's physical development, had his nursery not provided this Forest School opportunity. There are also emotional consequences around his perceptions of safety. As long ago as 2003, Jennie Lindon was warning of the dangers to children that come from over-protection in the preschool years (Lindon, 2003: 10), and suggesting that children need to take age-appropriate risks in order to learn to stay safe. Gill (2007) followed this up by focusing on the same issues but mainly around the needs of school-aged children. He considered the demise of adventure playgrounds in inner cities during the 1970s and 1980s, such as the one in Figure 2.1 that still survives in London, and asked us to consider what this says about our attitudes to children. Are they 'fragile, incompetent, accident-prone, unable to deal with adversity and incapable of learning how to look after themselves' (ibid.: 38)? In Forest School, the attitude is one of mutual trust and shared learning, which is why tool use and fire lighting are common activities, regardless of the ages of the children.

In his literature review, Gill (2014) finds not only that playful engagements with nature are beneficial to young children, but also that it is the urban poor who are the least likely to experience this kind of engagement. Case Study 2.1 documents how funding is being sought to counter this in the London Borough of Hackney, as the organisers are already seeing benefits to children's confidence and communication skills from being outside. It is these social skills, so important to later academic success, that have been recorded as being improved through sustained attendance at Forest School sessions. The earliest research observations of Forest School activities (Borradaile, 2006; Hughes, 2007; O'Brien and Murray, 2007) reported on the evidence of the impact of Forest School on children's sense of well-being, on their communication skills and on their ability to engage in social interactions. Case Study 2.2 records an example of just such a development in a very young boy, building confidence and physical prowess. Fortunately, there are settings springing up around all the major conurbations in the UK. A quick glance at the database on the FSA

FIGURE 2.2   An Adventure Playground in London

website (FSA, 2016a), for example, reveals six within the London Orbital Motorway, the M25, eight in Birmingham, two in Newcastle, and one each in Edinburgh and Glasgow. As not everyone registers on the map, it is likely that there are considerably more. For example, in London, as well as the subject of Case Study 2.1, there is another North London nursery, 'Into The Woods', rated outstanding in 2015 by Ofsted, as is 'The Woodland Nursery' in South-East London. 'Wild Education' runs Forest School activities in Twickenham, Kew, Sheen Common woods and Barnes Common. These are just a few examples, and more can be found by contacting the local authorities in each area.

Why wooded areas are so important to Forest School is a theme that will recur in many chapters. Nanson (2014: 149) speaks of the power of the wild-wood as linking humankind to deep time and the force of nature. Waters (2011) describes the importance of linking trees and stories to deepen children's understandings of nature. Cartwright (2012: 152) recounts how informal education, rooted in 'place', draws out knowledge rather than pouring it in, thus creating confidence and self-worth. Putting these ideas together gives a strong sense of the trees as partners in supporting the developing minds and bodies of children, helping them to feel safely rooted in their environments. Think back to your childhood and consider the importance of trees in your emotional growing.

Case Study 2.2 is of a partnership of two childminders that highlights another positive aspect of Forest School, which is that it does seem to be a way of enabling men to work more easily with preschool children. This issue has been discussed at length, from debating feminine and masculine discourses in settings (Osgood, 2008) to the discrimination faced by male workers as a result of public perceptions of childcare as 'women's work' (Bligh et al., 2013: 103). Whilst a quick overview at the 2015 Forest School conference of those practitioners engaged in working with the youngest children reinforced the stereotypical gender divide, Forest School does seem less prone to such extremes than indoor settings. For example, in this part of the book, there are six case study settings and in three of them there are male childcare workers engaged in Forest School. This is good news for the children and for the workface. As Martin (2012: 41) states: 'representational politics around gender equity tend to simplify and distort issues involved with school achievement'. It is not just that all children need good role models who they can identify with, it is more that they are growing up around adults who share the tasks of fire lighting, tool use, story telling, etc., in the spirit of Forest School Principles 3 and 4, to create a community for well-being, development and learning, and to promote the holistic development of all of those involved. This encourages all children to realise their own potential and to confidently engage with whatever interests them.

In Case Study 2.2, Mike and Charissa have taken the decision to drive out of the city of Bristol to a wood, but this is not the only solution to finding urban wooded spaces. The subject of Case Study 2.1 is just one of the settings that has found a park with a wooded area. As can be seen in Figure 2.3, many parks have such areas and those managing them may be amenable to allowing groups of very young children in to use them for Forest School. The only disadvantage to using such spaces is that it is rarely possible to light fires. If that is the only option available, then it is better to use the space than deprive the children. It may be possible to renegotiate the situation after you have proved to be model users of the space!

The advantage of starting with a wooded space in a park with very young children is that woods can be scary. As Bryson (1997: 61) says of woods: 'Their trees surround you, loom over you, press in from all sides … And they are alive.' They are alive, and eventually the children need to encounter them in the wild. But, for urban children, meeting them in a relatively tamed space can be a useful starting point. Here, they can learn to love them as individuals and respect them as creatures in need of water, nourishment and light, not to mention our care and consideration. This is the first step towards a sustainable future – sustainable for the children and sustainable for the trees.

FIGURE 2.3   A Forest School Session in a Park

GOING FORWARD

REFLECTIONS ON FOREST SCHOOL

This chapter has noted the advances towards gender equality in early years Forest School practice. The equality issue that has not as yet been successfully addressed is that of 'race'. Despite our islands having been populated by people of African origin since Roman times and by people whose roots were in the Indian subcontinent for over a thousand years, and despite being a hotchpotch of peoples at all times (Cole, 2012: 79), it was sad to note that at the 2015 FSA conference the number of delegates of obviously non-white ethnic origins could be counted on the fingers of one hand. This was discussed by delegates at a previous conference but as yet no one seems to have found a way of attracting a more ethnically diverse range of trainees into the sector. Reflect on why this might be and how the situation might be made more representative of the population at large.

IDEAS FOR PRACTICE: TREE CLIMBING

Once upon a time, all children and many adults climbed trees. Children still have the urge to be higher and see further, as well as to find that secret space where they can see and not be seen. Only trees will do. Climbing frames are sterile imitations with evenly spaced rungs that eliminate challenge and destroy mystery. If you never climbed a tree as a child, try it now. You will find, as children do, that your natural ability will limit how high you feel confident going. And adults don't bounce like children do, nor do their bones mend as easily, so listen to your inner voice. But if you are working with children who want to climb, then find ways to help them get started. Many just want to start off by being lifted into a fork in the branches to experience being higher and feeling the living tree move with the breeze. They will not imitate kittens and climb till they are stuck. Actually, unless frightened, kittens won't climb too high, either, and children can be talked down if they lose confidence at a critical point.

FURTHER READING

- At the time of writing, this book is still in press, but promises to be a cross between a how-to guide and 'a daydreamer's handbook', according to publishers HarperCollins. *The Treeclimber's Guide to London* (2016) by Jack Cooke could help urban Forest School leaders to find their way to climbable trees.
- *Plants for Play* by Robin Moore (Berkeley, CA: MIG Communications,1993) will help you to work out how to use the plants in the park, or, indeed, which to teach the children to avoid. It will also give you ideas for your gardens, hanging baskets and window ledges. It was published in the USA, so the guidance on frost tolerance is less helpful, but the plant lists are a great source of ideas.
- Professor Moore has also been instrumental in writing some guidelines for American parks which are a useful download: Moore, R. (2015) *Nature Play and Learning Places*. Raleigh, NC: Natural Learning Initiative; and Reston, VA: National Wildlife Federation, available at https://natureplayandlearningplaces.org/

3

Rural Day Nurseries

The case studies in this chapter are of two daycare settings, examples of where the proprietors place a great deal of importance on getting children outside, and are in rural settings with extensive access to the outdoors. The children in both spend long periods of time outside, and can often move freely between indoors and outside, responding to their own intrinsic motivations. Sarah and Alison would both recognise Claire Warden's nature pedagogy as their own aspiration for nature as the 'stream underneath' (Warden, 2015) that underpins the experiences of the children in their care.

CASE STUDY 3.1: SMALL STEPS DAY CARE

Hidden away up a country lane miles from any towns and nestling up to the farm run by the setting's proprietors, Small Steps Day Care is very rural. It was established in 2007 and is managed by its proprietor, Sarah Roe. Small Steps cares for preschool children aged 2–5 years during term time and children up to 8 years of age for occasional care, for example on teacher training days. During the summer holidays, they run a holiday club instead of the daily sessions. Children attend for full days, morning or afternoon sessions, or for shorter hours. Small Steps is Ofsted-registered and was inspected in January 2015, when it was rated 'Outstanding' in all three areas.

(Continued)

(Continued)

The building is modern and light with big windows. The patio doors of the main room open directly onto the garden, which has a raised-bed vegetable-growing area with composting facilities (see Figure 3.1), a sensory area planted with aromatic herbs and flowers, a large poultry run inhabited by an array of chickens and a couple of turkeys, a sandpit under a willow arbour, a tipi and a mud kitchen, as well as the usual play house, bikes, cars and trucks. Piles of tyres and milk crates provide the 'loose parts', as do odd pieces of wood and brick. As the garden extends towards open fields, the grass becomes longer and lumpier with a fallen tree to climb, a mound of earth and an assortment of objects such as insect houses and concrete model castles – anything that might stimulate the imagination of a young child and looking as if they had decided on its location. The doors open into the outdoors at 9.30 am and stay open, the children moving freely between indoors and out.

Young trees planted when the setting opened are growing well on the south-western side of the fence between the children and the parking area. South-east, a chainlink fence separates the setting from the farm but the children enjoy frequent excursions across the fields, nature watching and observing seasonal farm work such as harvesting. Sarah looks to incorporate these extended outdoor activities into the day as often as possible, citing the positive effects on her own children as the motivator for her belief in the health and educational benefits of being outdoors. Tool use, for example cutting tough sunflower stems with an axe, is encouraged, as is time for lying in the grass, making grass angels and staring at the clouds in the sky.

The curriculum is based on observations of children's interests and led by knowledge of their developmental needs. The children are decision makers, partners and confident risk-takers. Any initial parental concerns are allayed by detailed newsletters that link what has happened to their developmental benefits. The atmosphere is relaxed, and one of harmonious appreciation of the natural world and its seasonal changes.

CASE STUDY 3.2: NATURE TRAILS DAY NURSERY

Nature Trails Day Nursery at Cawston, Rugby, opened in November 2004. It is situated in purpose-built accommodation overlooking woodland and open countryside, and caters for children from 6 months to preschool age between the hours of 8 am and 6 pm, Monday to Friday. The children are grouped by age, as a response to English registration requirements for different ratios of adults to children at different ages. However, there are times each day when the children can mingle more freely. The curriculum and practice reflect the Department for Education's Early Years Foundation Stage guidance and Statutory Framework requirements (DfE 2014a). Nevertheless, the learning ethos is also influenced by European models of nursery education that emphasise the importance of play, exploration and enjoyment of learning. The nursery director, Alison Dyke, feels passionate about taking very young children out into the woodland and into natural environments.

Initially, the nursery was in a small building attached to an old farmhouse. Since 2004, it has expanded and there are now four units: two situated in the main building, whilst Forest Friends Preschool is located in two adjoining purpose-built log cabins. In 2015, Ofsted rated the setting as 'Outstanding'. There is a variety of different outdoor play areas, including two all-weather surfaced gardens and small covered verandas that enable children to play outdoors whatever the weather, if they wish. All children make use of the surrounding countryside and the local woods. Free-flow outdoor learning is available for all children in the log cabin areas and there are play areas with mud kitchens and planting areas, as well as space for more conventional bikes and trikes. When children reach the year prior to commencing school, they attend Forest School sessions once a week in an orchard belonging to the main farmhouse. From there, they have direct access via a gate to the lane and woodland that lie beyond the nursery. The children are able to climb trees, make dens, explore nature, build with natural materials, use tools and occasionally cook on open fires. The nursery staff find that children who behave and learn in one way in a traditional classroom environment do not necessarily behave in the same way outside: often, a quiet child will 'come out of their shell' when outside, while a more exuberant child may calm down and show more awareness of themselves and their impact on the environment.

All the nursery practitioners are introduced to the principles of Forest School and undertake induction training which ensures that they use the countryside environment to its full potential, wisely and with the children's best learning and safety interests at heart. This means that by the time that children reach preschool age, they show a respect for the countryside and wildlife and demonstrate a high level of confidence and a passion for playing outdoors.

Small Steps, in Case Study 3.1, does not claim to offer Forest School, and yet the children there are deeply engaged in the countryside around them, some of which is wooded. It is one of several daycare settings across the UK that is based on a farm and that uses its farm as a resource for the children in creative and meaningful ways. If the FSA Principles and Criteria for Good Practice (FSA, 2011) are considered, then Sarah's children are experiencing four of the six on a daily basis, however Sarah is not trained as a Forest School practitioner and was concerned about how her provision would be viewed by the Forest School community because of that. What she does have is a lifetime of knowledge and love of the natural world, her knowledge and experience as a farmer and her knowledge and experience as an early years professional. She is not one of the lost generation of adults lacking in contact with the natural world during her growing up. Her skills, knowledge and experience combine to enable her to create an environment that arguably has equal value for these very young children as a Forest School setting, albeit one perhaps more correctly labelled as 'Farm School' or, indeed, 'Nature Kindergarten'.

In Case Study 3.2, Alison, too, has her own depth of knowledge, skills and experience, but her setting caters for many more children and from just a few months old, so she employs a significant number of staff to deliver the day-to-day care and education for the children. Some of her staff are Forest School-trained and take the older children off-site to the nearby wooded spaces to enjoy the full Forest School experience. This is not to detract from the valuable work being done on-site with the mud kitchen, the growing areas and pet care. All the children have an opportunity to engage deeply with their natural surroundings, to use tools and to light fires. With a larger staff, she does find that the natural turnover of personnel can leave her without Level 3 FS-trained staff for short periods, and that other staff lack the confidence to step in, even in the short term, to support the children in natural outdoor play. They appear to see the training as a magic ticket to certainty and competence in all areas of outdoor learning, rather than something specific to wilder and wooded experiences.

These very different settings represent a tension in the early years sector, in England in particular, but with repercussions across all the home nations of the UK. Whilst the 2008 Foundation Stage Guidance explicitly mentioned outdoor provision and its importance, this was relaxed in England in the 2014 changes to allow for more flexibility. Inevitably, this has led to some settings seeing outdoor provision as being less of a priority. In addition, the new Early Years Professional Status conferred on graduates has enabled practitioners with less practical experience to achieve a management role at a very early stage in their career. Add to that the aforementioned generational experiential gap and there is the possibility that the ground gained by the inspiration that the expansion of Forest School in the noughties provided to settings will now be lost as some settings hide behind the lack of outdoor qualified staff to deliver Forest School or any other forms of outdoor experiences to our youngest children, just at the time in their development when they would benefit the most. In these case study settings, both of which are rural and both of which are led by experienced staff committed to outdoor learning, one can see this tension in practice.

A dangerous result from this tension would be to see Forest School as a constraining influence rather than an inspiring one, as practitioners hide behind their lack of Forest School training as an excuse for not engaging in any outdoor learning. It has always been the case that it is the adults rather than the children who have been reluctant to go outside, with reasons stated variously as weather, temperature, mud, etc. One possible course of action would be a requirement to include nature education as a part of early years training, but that would need action at a governmental level. In some universities and colleges across the home nations, this is happening, as can be seen in Part 2 of this book, but at present it is not a universal requirement and therefore not a universal entitlement for students. Another course of action is for those practitioners who are inspired to go outside to engage with parents to ensure that as many as possible of the next generation are not caught in the nature-deficit bind. Parental pressure has been behind the 'Project Wild Thing' campaign in the UK (www.thewildnetwork.com/), the National Trust's 'Fifty Things To Do Before You Are 11¾' (www.50things.org.uk/) and books such as *Go Wild* (Schofield and Danks, 2009). It would seem that parents are concerned by the paucity of outdoor experiences that their young children encounter, but lack the confidence themselves to rectify the situation without help.

What should be the goal? As Davis (2015: 15) states, young children are disproportionately affected by the impacts of global warming, and they will be the inheritors of the sustainability issues affecting the planet. It is therefore the duty of early years educators to equip them to deal with their inheritance. All settings need to be doing as our case study settings are, and acquainting children as closely as possible with the world around them. Elinor Goldschmied (Jackson & Forbes, 2015) pointed the way with her work on 'treasure baskets', highlighting the importance of time and space for babies and toddlers to explore natural objects in their worlds and understand the nature of those objects in that world. Fears about the risks to them from, say, chewing on a fir cone need to be rationalised and understood as reasonable and a part of the learning process. My mother told me that she knew I would be creative because as a baby I stuffed daisies up my nose whilst my sister ate worms. Neither of us suffered. From those first explorations, toddlers progress to digging, mixing and exploring in the outside environment and gain a strong sense of their own agency and impact on that world. Growing food and feeding other creatures give that agency morality and responsibility. These should be every preschool child's entitlement. It is the foundation for their sense of self as an active and integral part of the world in which they live. Without it, there is a danger that children will grow into passive and accepting bigger children rather than becoming adults, reliant on others to make decisions for them, uncaring about the creatures that share their world and quick to blame others when things go wrong for them.

If the experiences of all children included what is essentially sensory and messy outdoor play and gardening, and there is no reason why this can't be achieved in all settings, then the pressure is lifted from Forest School training to legitimise such everyday experiences, and Forest School training can focus on a different kind of outdoor learning. To deprive any child of learning about the natural world around them in the early stages of their development truly is nature-deficit disorder (Louv, 2009: 10), a condition that will stunt them physically, socially, emotionally and spiritually. When young, all children need to be outside in nature as much as possible, as can be seen in the case studies in this chapter. This doesn't require special training, only an open mind and a commitment to do what is in children's best interests.

FIGURE 3.1   Small Steps Day Care Growing Area

Forest School is less about nature and more about wild. It is what Barnes (2007: 92) calls our need for wildness which feeds us spiritually and emotionally at a deeper level. It is something that can be important at any age. Indeed, it can be one way of helping people to overcome the effects of early nature deprivation, which is why trees are such useful allies in the re-wilding process. Tudge (2006: 369) states that: 'Trees are right at the heart of all the necessary debates: ecological, social, economic, political, moral, religious.' Most people respond positively to trees, whether that positivity expresses itself in a desire to climb, shelter, hug or contemplate. At a species level, we respond to these living beings that sheltered and provided for us through millennia, and which still do (Sempik et al., 2010: 89). Forest School training enables practitioners to work with trees to improve lives. For young children, it is about widening their experiential pool and deepening their resilience to the rigours of modern life. It builds on their entitlement to access to nature; it does not replace it.

GOING FORWARD

REFLECTIONS ON FOREST SCHOOL

It would appear that a good early years setting can provide outdoor experiences of high quality to our youngest children without needing Forest School training. This enables Forest School practitioners to reflect on what it is that is additional about Forest School. The nature of a naturally wooded environment and the quality of the training that practitioners undertake would seem to be key to this additionality. The quality of training will be discussed in the next part, so take the opportunity now to reflect on the nature of trees and our relationship with them. Consider the myths, legends and stories that include trees. For instance, the Norse Yggdrasil, the Buddhist Bo Tree and the Islamic Tree of Immortality are three examples of religious trees, and Christian theologians speak of the Tree of Life. Children's stories include *Hansel and Gretel* and *Little Red Riding Hood*. Shakespeare uses the forest for magical purposes (*A Midsummer Night's Dream*) and as a place of safety to hide in (*As You Like It*). What does this tell you about humans and trees?

IDEAS FOR PRACTICE: PAINTING WITH MUD

Mark making is a human urge and develops a range of skills which will be useful later in learning both writing and reading. In the photograph in Figure 3.2, a young child relishes the opportunity to 'paint' on a piece of cloth with mud. The tray before him contains a range of rollers, paint pots, different-sized brushes; and containers for him to use to mix further compounds and put other 'brushes' such as sticks and leaves. There are potentially rich outcomes from this activity, including:

- an appreciation of different viscosities of mud and the language to describe them
- an appreciation of the different colours of soil types and the language to describe them

FIGURE 3.2   Painting with Mud

- improved hand–eye coordination
- development of creativity and imagination
- invention of a story for the picture
- consideration of what makes a good mark-making implement.

These artistic endeavours feed into all forms of creativity including painting, writing and communication.

FURTHER READING

- Explore the importance of nature to children by reading Richard Louv's (2009) book *Last Child in the Woods*, and then explore the added element of wildness with a book such as Simon Barnes' (2007) *How to be Wild*. What do such passionate writings tell you about the importance of both outdoor learning and Forest School?
- Consider how young children acquire education for sustainability and how important this will be for their future. Davis's (2015) book *Young Children and the Environment* will help you, particularly Chapter 2 by Sue Elliott.
- Consider some of the theories that relate to the pedagogy of Forest School. A recent chapter I wrote will give you leads from its references (Knight, 2016a).

Part 2

Forest School Opportunities for 3–5 Year Olds

4

Scotland

This chapter looks at the development of Forest School in Scotland and in particular how it is being used with 3–5-year-olds. It will start by describing the central role played by the Forestry Commission in Scotland in supporting the introduction of Forest School, as, indeed, it has done across the whole of Great Britain. It will also consider the relationship between the Curriculum for Excellence (Education Scotland 2010) and Forest School, and what the implications are for the future. In particular, it will reflect on the possible impact that the requirements of the General Teaching Council for Scotland for evidence of continuing professional development (CPD) could have on training for the delivery of Forest School. The case studies will be of two of the practitioners who have been instrumental in spreading Forest School for 3–5-year-olds across Scotland.

The Forestry Commission Scotland (FCS) played a very active part in establishing the delivery of Forest School across the country, as can be seen in Case Study 4.1. Given that the FCS owns 9 per cent of the land mass in Scotland, this has been essential for the development of Forest School. Through its education arm, first known as the Forest Education Initiative (FEI) and then from 2014 as Outdoor and Woodland Learning (OWL) Scotland, a national Forest School coordinator has supported the strategic development of Forest School by forming local groups, developing and sharing resources, and populating the website with publicity and useful information (http://owlscotland.org/). Events, links and funding opportunities ensured that Forest School established a firm base in Scotland, and the Forestry Commission commissioned and then encouraged the publication of early research data such as 'Forest School Scotland: An Evaluation' (Borradaile, 2006), a report on outcomes for 3–5-year-olds. As in the majority of the home nations, it was this preschool group that benefitted first and across most areas of the country. However, following recessions in the late noughties, reorganisations and cuts have led to this leadership role being considerably curtailed. From a funded post, it is now largely delegated to the group coordinators who have voluntary time only in which to keep the flow of news alive through the OWL website. If Forest School had not proved itself to be successful, not only through the publication of reports and case studies but also through the direct experience of early years professionals, teachers and parents, the diminution of the Forestry Commission role could have had catastrophic results. Fortunately, this has not been the case, and Forest School continues to thrive, as can be seen in Case Study 4.2.

CASE STUDY 4.1: PENNY MARTIN

Already an experienced outdoor learning practitioner, Penny trained as a Forest School leader early in the noughties and became the Scotland Forest School Coordinator in 2010. This was a part-time post, and she continued to practise as an independent Outdoor Learning consultant and Forest School practitioner alongside this. The post of coordinator was hosted by Living Classrooms, the charitable arm of Mindstretchers plc, and funded through Forestry Commission Scotland (FCS)'s Forests for People and Forest Development Programme funding. Her role was to evaluate and support the strategic development of Forest School in Scotland, through the Forest Education Initiative (FEI) – now known as Outdoor & Woodland Learning (OWL) Scotland – and its local groups. Day to day, this included responding to enquiries, supporting the Forest School practitioner and trainer network across Scotland, and linking to developments across the UK. It also included being a part of the group of practitioners who contributed to the Forest School Association in the UK in 2012, travelling south to meetings in Birmingham and London to articulate the Scottish perspective. She has developed and shared resources via the OWL Scotland website and developed the FS Scotland database. Action plans were also made to put this work into a strategic framework. Away from the desk, web-based case studies were inspired by Forest School site visits across Scotland, three of which are available on the OWL Scotland website (OWL Scotland, 2015), and she supported national and local events and delivered workshops with FCS and partner organisations. Since the funding for the post closed in December 2014, she has left the Forest School network in Scotland on a stronger footing, with more supporting resources available and now better integrated into the wider Outdoor & Woodland Learning context for Scotland.

As an independent practitioner and consultant, Penny has been successful in obtaining ongoing and repeat contract work with a range of clients, including Forestry Commission Scotland, Scottish Natural Heritage, Grounds for Learning, the Woodland

Trust and RSPB, and, more recently, project-based work with Perthshire Women's Aid. Work has included the development and writing of educational resources, research reviews, biodiversity resources, school grounds developments, training and workshop delivery, and event planning and management. Most recently, this included the development and delivery of the 2015 launch event for Outdoor & Woodland Learning Scotland. She is also treasurer for and an active member of the Tayside OWL Group. In April 2015, Penny secured a part-time post as Environment & Forestry (ENFOR) Outdoor Learning Project Officer. This role included continued support for Forest School Scotland enquiries and database management, and the development of the Outdoor Learning Directory, an ENFOR partner website providing a portal to outdoor learning resources across Scotland. She is involved in co-delivering Forest School programmes for Perthshire Women's Aid client groups as a Big Lottery Communities & Families Fund/Tayside OWL project.

CASE STUDY 4.2: ALINE HILL

Aline is based in Fife and has been facilitating creative outdoor learning, including Forest School, with a diverse range of children and young people in Edinburgh and the Lothians since 2005. Aline sat on both the FEI Scotland Trainer's Network and FEI Scotland Forest School Working Group prior to their reorganisations, and runs her own company, BigWorld, as well as being a trainer with the Forest School Training Cooperative. She works within the Forest School model, which ensures good practice in relation to holistic child development, policies and procedures and environmental sustainability.

Aline fell in love with the magic of Forest School and its potential to reconnect people and nature, transforming learning, lives, communities and landscapes, 10 years ago, having had a previous life in publishing and university lecturing. She stepped down as vice-chair of the Forest School Association in October 2015, having served as a founding director since 2012. Through her work to support early years and primary settings in developing elemental natural play opportunities, she continues to contextualise Forest School within the wider field of outdoor learning and is always delighted to support early years practitioners through the Forest School training journey. Over the years, she has worked in partnership with many organisations, including the Scottish Department for Education, Forestry Commission Scotland, East Lothian Council, Edinburgh Outdoor and Woodland Learning, City of Edinburgh Council, Borders Forest Trust, Inspirationally Wild, FEI North East Fife, South Lanarkshire Council, Glasgow Countryside Ranger Service, and New Caledonian Woodland.

Aline has embraced the common model of outdoor work described by Allin and West (2016: 162) as a boundaryless career – less of a linear progression to a perceived peak, and more an ever-expanding ripple of competencies and experiences that create a valuable member of the Forest School Community.

OWL Scotland continues to support Forest School on its website with links to local groups and a map of Forest School activity in Scotland (OWL Scotland, 2014). As a part of the public service offered by OWL Scotland, it includes a summary table of the different ways in which children and young people can access outdoor and woodland learning. There are in Scotland a range of possibilities for children in the key 3–5 age range as well as for older children and adults, with Forest School and Forest Kindergarten being those identified as requiring access to trees or woodland.

Forest Kindergarten was developed by the Forestry Commission in 2009 in response to the Scottish Index of Multiple Deprivation (SIMD), first published in 2009 and updated subsequently (Scottish Government, 2015), which identifies small area concentrations of multiple deprivation across the whole of Scotland in a statistically homogeneous way to ensure interagency access to the data. This allows for effective targeting of policies and funding where the aim is to wholly or partly tackle the effects of deprivation on children's development, or take account of area concentrations of multiple deprivation when taking policy decisions about where to allocate resources. The Forestry Commission Scotland has used this opportunity to develop a three-day course for early years professionals in central Scotland to encourage them to improve the outdoor experiences that they offer in those areas identified by the SIMD as having high levels of deprivation. Whilst this three-day course does not cover the full scope of the Forest School leadership award, its existence acknowledges the effectiveness of Forest School. It will be interesting to see how this initiative is supported in the 2016 Strategic Plan. In the plan for 2013–16, there were commitments to outdoor learning (FCS, 2013: 37) and a specific mention of Forest School: 'We will continue to work with education and health initiatives like Forest Education Initiative, Forest School and Branching Out' (ibid.: 51).

Another option mentioned on the OWL website is Nature Kindergarten. This was mentioned in Chapter 1 as an initiative spearheaded by Mindstretchers, and is the descriptor used by Claire Warden for the Auchlone setting described in Case Study 1.1. The training offered by Mindstretchers encourages a Forest School type environment in early years settings outdoors, is being offered across the world, and is described in Warden (2012). Again, Forest School has been the inspiration for creating a way to enable every early years setting to feel confident to allow children to be outside for longer and for that experience to be properly valued as a part of the curriculum.

Scotland has a long tradition of quality education and has always had its own distinct system, even before devolution in 1999. The Curriculum for Excellence (2004) has been a further step along this road, with modifications continuing. This embeds a more pupil-centred and holistic approach to learning, looking at 'capacities', similar to the 'dispositions' proposed by Claxton (2005). In Scotland, children do not usually start formal education until they are 5 years old, although the flexible entrance policy in Scotland allows for eligibility to start school when they are aged between 4.5 and 5.5 years old and at a time appropriate to them within that year. There is curriculum guidance for childcare professionals for pre-birth to 3 years of age, and the Curriculum for Excellence applies to children aged 3–18, with an emphasis on play-based learning in the early years (preschool and P1, which covers children aged 5–6).

Outdoor learning is explicitly embedded as a key component of the curriculum, and, since the introduction of the Curriculum for Excellence, there has been a steady increase of pressure on teachers to integrate outdoor learning into their delivery model: 'The core values of Curriculum for Excellence echo the key concepts of outdoor learning: challenge, enjoyment, relevance, depth, development of the whole person and an adventurous approach to learning' (Education Scotland, 2010). It is in the early years that the greatest progress has been made (Christie et al., 2016: 116) and it would appear that Forest School has been an influence on this progress. Whereas at secondary level the majority of outdoor experiences have remained within the traditional model of adventure education or residential trips (Christie et al., 2014), at primary level the model is more likely to be a place-based socio-ecological approach which fits with the rise of importance of teaching for sustainability in the curriculum. This is made explicit in FS Principle 2, which states that: 'Forest School aims to foster a relationship with nature through regular personal experiences in order to develop long-term, environmentally sustainable attitudes and practices in staff, learners and the wider community' (FSA, 2011). It also demands different roles from classroom teachers who, instead of handing over the delivery of the outdoor curriculum to experts to teach and/or instruct, are in this model a part of the community of learners and co-teachers. This has implications for teacher training.

As in the other home nations, teaching is a graduate-led profession, requiring either a BA (Hons) in Primary Education, a Post Graduate Diploma in Education (PGDE) or an MA (Hons) Education (Primary) or equivalent. Teaching children with Additional Support Needs requires further study. Once initially trained, there is a one-year probationary period. This is the same across the home nations. After this, teachers in Scotland are registered with the General Teaching Council for Scotland (GTCS). Since 2014, the GTCS has required teachers to engage with a professional updating process (GTC Scotland, 2014), necessitating an annual reflective account of CPD which feeds into a five-yearly confirmation with the GTCS of their registration as teachers. This reflective account needs teachers to link their own professional development to plans for whole-school development and improvement. When the curriculum requires outdoor experiences and when the regulatory authorities require evidence of CPD and planning for improvement, then there is a pressure on teachers to gain knowledge and experience of age-appropriate outdoor learning pedagogies.

Added to this, are the requirements of the CfE to include outdoor activities that are '"spontaneous" or pre-planned, "off-the-shelf" local visits when, for example, weather conditions are suitable or favourable' (Education Scotland, 2010: 13) and that 'deliver sustainable development education through initiatives such as working to improve biodiversity in the school grounds, visiting the local woods, exploring and engaging with the local community and developing a school travel plan' (ibid.: 15). Forest School is quoted directly as one way of achieving this (ibid.). Partnership working is encouraged but on a continuum from remote advisory role through to handing over to partners for planning and leading, requiring all class teachers in early years and primary education to engage with outdoor learning in some way or another. As can be seen from the case studies, Forest School leaders have been working across this continuum within a range of settings, however the professional updating requirements for teachers may extend this role. Of all the home nations, it is currently Scotland where teachers in the early years are most likely to encounter Forest School as a part of their initial training, although this may soon happen more consistently in Wales, as we will see in the next chapter. At Strathclyde and Edinburgh Universities in 2015, there were discussions as to how to include outdoor training that will prepare young teachers to be able to deliver parts of the outdoor curriculum. It would seem that in Scotland at least, the future of Forest School is assured.

GOING FORWARD

REFLECTIONS ON FOREST SCHOOL

If Forest School-like training is embedded into early years teacher training in Scotland, or if early primary school teachers are encouraged to undertake Forest School training as a part of their CPD, there is a danger that the ethos and principles of FS could be subsumed into the other demands of the curriculum. The tensions can be identified by a triangulation of three documents: the Forest School Principles (FSA, 2011), the 'Curriculum for Excellence through Outdoor Learning' (Education Scotland, 2010) and the 'Curriculum for Excellence: Assessing progress and achievement in the 3–15 broad general education' (Education Scotland, 2012). Whilst the CfE raises hopes and aspirations in the hearts of Forest School practitioners, it is good to critically examine these documents and reflect on how they may intersect.

IDEAS FOR PRACTICE: BLACKBERRY PANCAKES (FIGURE 4.1)

1   The principle idea is to encourage children to eat fruit growing seasonally and plentifully in their environment and blackberries are one of the fruits most likely to fall into this category.

2   Encourage the children to harvest their own fruit from a location high enough not to be sprayed by dogs and away from polluting car fumes.

3   Depending on location and season, blackberries are readily variable, but children can experiment with whatever you have collectively located and agreed is safe to eat. Do not be surprised if they experiment with unlikely flavours such as tomato pancakes, if that is what you have growing locally. In Scotland, you may also be lucky enough to find wild raspberries, cloudberries or blueberries.

4   A batter mix can be carried out to the camp fire in a plastic water container. A 2-litre container will make at least 10 small pancakes.

5   When the pancake is cooked, the child can sprinkle their fruit on it, then the pancake needs to be folded like a wrap, so that the fruit doesn't fall out when the pancake is picked up and eaten.

FIGURE 4.1   Blackberry Pancakes

FURTHER READING

- As a critique of recent practice, the paper (Christie et al., 2014) cited above is helpful. These authors, collectively and separately, are responsible for valuable research in the field of outdoor education, and it is good to note that their attention is now including the early part of the primary curriculum.
- Building Learning Power grew from research by Professor Guy Claxton into how children learn. Although it does not focus on outdoor learning, its messages are useful for Forest School practitioners. As well as the book (Claxton, 2005) cited in this chapter, there is a Building Learning Power website (www.tloltd.co.uk/building-learning-power/) with further information and links.
- Claire Warden has been mentioned several times in this book so far. Her latest book (Warden, 2015) has been cited previously and will be a useful read for Forest School and early years leaders.

5
Wales

In the same way as we saw in Scotland in the previous chapter, the Forestry Commission has played a leading role in developing Forest School in Wales, in particular for children aged 3–5 years. And again, as in Scotland, curriculum developments in Wales have also contributed to this. The relationship between the curriculum as developed by the Welsh Assembly Government and the Forest School as developed by the Forestry Commission is the central consideration of this chapter. The case study will illuminate how interagency working has led to developments in training which will shape this relationship in the next few years, and help Forest School to retain its identity and importance in the principality.

In 2010, the Welsh Assembly Government launched The Foundation Phase of the National Curriculum in Wales as the statutory curriculum for all 3–7-year-olds. This is different from the other curricula in the British Isles in that it explicitly identifies the early years as a distinct phase of learning through to the age of 7. This echoes the alleged Jesuit claim from the 17th century: 'Give me a child until he is seven and I will give you the man,' the age identified by Jean Piaget as the pre-operational stage of development from the early 20th century when children learn best through play, as in Figure 5.1, and the pre-preparatory stage of the English private school system when historically children were taught at home. It also reflects the starting age for compulsory schooling in many countries across Europe.

FIGURE 5.1   European School Starting Ages

Age (years)	Countries
4	Northern Ireland
5	England, Scotland, Wales, Malta
5.5	Cyprus, Macedonia, Turkey
6	Austria, Belgium, Bosnia and Herzegovina, Croatia, Czech Republic, Denmark, France, Germany, Greece, Hungary, Iceland, Republic of Ireland, Italy, Liechtenstein, Luxembourg, Montenegro, Netherlands, Norway, Poland, Portugal, Romania, Serbia, Slovakia, Slovenia, Spain, Switzerland, Turkey
7	Bulgaria, Croatia, Estonia, Finland, Latvia, Lithuania, Poland, Sweden

Source: European Commission et al. (2015)

As can be seen in Figure 5.1, it is misleading to take the compulsory school starting age as a definite indicator of when a formal style of teaching and learning is adopted, as all of the UK home nations have early compulsory school starting ages. However, in the previous chapter, we considered the Scottish Curriculum for Excellence which advocates play-based and/or active learning in the early primary years (Learning and Teaching Scotland, 2007: 10). But it is an indicator of trends and the Pan-European trend is not in line with the UK education systems. This is one of the reasons for which I discussed why Forest School was taken up with such enthusiasm by practitioners working with 3–5-year-olds (Knight, 2016c) offering at the outset of its introduction in the late 1990s a counter to the advancing tide of formalisation in UK early years policy. The link between Forestry Commission Wales and the developing Welsh curriculum has reinforced a counter-trend in Wales. This has led to an extensive programme of training for Foundation Phase staff in Forest School practice (Natural Resources Wales, 2015: 14). The perception of one university lecturer in Cardiff is that in the capital city, nine out of ten schools had Forest School leaders active in them in 2015.

The Foundation Phase was revised by the Department for Education and Skills (DfES) of the Welsh Government in 2015, to be phased in from the start of that academic year. This followed the Donaldson Review of the curriculum, published in February 2015 (Donaldson, 2015). Unlike the Alexander Review in

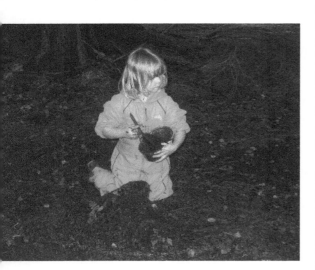

FIGURE 5.2   Forest School in Wales

England in 2009 (Alexander et al., 2010), the recommendations of Professor Donaldson and his team seem to have been accepted, allowing the potential for a more flexible, creative and individualised curriculum offer. The introduction states that the 'Foundation Phase environment should promote discovery and independence and a greater emphasis on using the outdoor environment as a resource for children's learning' (DfES, 2015: 3), continuing the link between curriculum delivery and the environment. The latest guidance states that the 'benefits of outdoor learning and play for children cannot be underestimated' (DfES, 2014: 12), and explicitly mentions 'regular opportunities to access Forest School' (ibid.: 4). What is interesting is that as practitioner confidence in delivering outdoor learning generally grows, so it is that Forest School is able to retain its unique identity as the wilder and more child-led part of the outdoor offering. This is reflected in the developments that have taken place in what the Forestry Commission Wales, now Natural Resources Wales, has to offer.

The histories of the various bodies such as the Forestry Commission and the Outdoor Learning Network are well documented on the internet as well as in a variety of documents issued by them. I have synthesised this information in an attempt to show how Forest School in Wales has been shaped by the people and politics of the principality. Case Study 5.1 is an example of the influence of one such person through more than one organisation.

CASE STUDY 5.1: AN INTERVIEW WITH CAROL TRAVERS

In October 2015, the author interviewed Carol Travers in her office in Abergavenny. Carol is the adult training lead in the Education, Learning and Sector Skills Team of Natural Resources Wales, which involves her in a wide range of environmental projects as well as curriculum-based outdoor education. She is also the Chair of the Outdoor Learning Training Network in Wales, and has been a key player in the development and support of Forest School in Wales. In these dual roles, she is interested in continuing to support Forest School whilst recognising that Outdoor Learning is wider and, in Wales, more pervasive within the curriculum.

We discussed the importance of continuing to give teachers and early years practitioners the confidence to embed play-based learning in the outdoors across the Foundation Phase and ways that this might be achieved. Carol explained that the Outdoor Learning Training Network in Wales is developing new Agored Cymru outdoor learning qualifications that embed Forest School into a family of outdoor training opportunities that will see the unique ethos of Forest School preserved; prior to this, there had been a risk that as Forest School training was the most readily available, trainees would call their outdoor learning practices Forest School even when

(Continued)

(Continued)

circumstances made it impossible to follow the ethos. At the time of writing, the first of these is now advertised on the Network website (www.outdoorlearningwales.org/outdoor-learning-training/outdoor-learning-training-network/), which also provides links to trainers and accredited courses. The training courses that Carol and the training network have developed are a combination of 'beyond the gate' provision – in other words, delivery that takes place outside the setting, for example in a forest or on a beach – and practice sited in the setting but outside, using natural resources and providing outdoor play activities. They will take two years to embed from 2015 as the new curriculum is rolled out, but will enable all practitioners to develop their practice to provide the outdoor opportunities demanded by the curriculum.

Carol has contacts in the Welsh universities and two are already delivering Forest School training to students on early years courses. She is hoping that this will continue to develop, as will CPD opportunities supported by local education officers. At present, the main demand for training is from early years staff, but the Donaldson Review (2015), already mentioned, has given her hope for the direction of travel in the statutory curriculum.

The Forest Education Initiative (FEI), a subsidiary of the Forestry Commission, was established in 1992 with the target of promoting education in and about wooded spaces. Bridgwater College launched its first Forest School in 1994. Local groups of people involved in outdoor learning, called cluster groups, were being constituted from 1995 in Wales, England and Scotland. The first FEI coordinator was appointed in 1996. Bridgwater College launched the first Forest School Level 3 training course that year. By the end of the 1990s, Forest School was on the radar of the FEI coordinator and sessions are now being run in the West of England and in Wales and Scotland. Training is being supported and in some cases funded by the FEI coordinator, who is helping local groups to bid for Forestry Commission grants.

The year 2000 saw the first FEI coordinator for South Wales appointed, quickly followed by one in North Wales the following year. In 2001, Bridgwater College ran the first Forest School Leader training course in South Wales. In 2002, members of the Forestry Commission Wales and Welsh college lecturers set about writing Forest School training courses specific to Wales. In 2003, the Open College Network (OCN) Wales ratified the Level 3 modules and OCN Level 1 and 2 courses were introduced in 2004. Also in 2003, the Forestry Commission devolved to become separate Forestry Commissions in Wales, Scotland and England. In Wales, the Woodlands for Learning Forum was created in 2003 with representation from FEI and from the new Wales Education Minister. In 2006, the Welsh Forest School Training Network was formed to represent all those trainers using the Welsh units (including English trainers using the Welsh units). Once again, it was the Forestry

Commission Wales that supported the formation of the group, and it was also advised by OCN Wales and two partner Further Education colleges – Coleg Gwent and the Welsh College of Horticulture. The Network enabled trainers to work together to address issues of concern and to start to build training capacity in Wales, and its first task was to revise the Level 3 units – those for the Forest School leadership award.

By the end of the decade, all three levels had been further revised and OCN Wales had become Agored Cymru, and completely independent from the UK-wide National OCN. In 2007, the Forestry Commission in Wales commissioned a DVD about Forest School delivery in Wales and secured Welsh Assembly funding to train Foundation Phase Forest School leaders. Thus, by the time the Foundation Phase was launched, there was a flourishing Forest School community with access to the ear of the Education Minister for Wales and supported by the Forestry Commission in the guise of the Forest Education Initiative (FEI). As we have seen, this encouraged practitioners in nurseries and schools to accept Forest School as an important part of the outdoor learning strategy in the Foundation Phase.

The years from 2010 to 2015 have seen further changes, amalgamations and devolutions. The FEI ceased to exist as a UK-wide body in 2012 and in 2013 Forestry Commission Wales became part of Natural Resources Wales, along with the Countryside Council for Wales and the Environment Agency in Wales, widening the remit to include more than just woodlands. As a consequence of this, in 2014, FEI Wales became Outdoor Learning Wales, also incorporating the learning opportunities of all natural habitats. The Trainers Network first expanded in 2007 to cover England and Scotland as well as Wales and then split to form the Wales Training Network and the Forest School Trainers Network GB, with representation from the Welsh network attending the GB meetings at least once a year. Forest School Wales (www. forestschoolwales.org.uk/) was formed, which is a voluntary organisation that coordinates skill sharing and CPD training opportunities and provides information about Forest School in Wales. The success of Forest School in Wales is surely due to the commitment of key people in the three organisations, which sometimes (as can be seen from the case study) are the same people wearing different hats, and the support of the Welsh Government in recognising the contribution Forest School can make to the healthy development of young children.

The reverse of the Welsh success story is that Forest School across the UK is more fragmented than is ideal for a young and vulnerable movement. Whilst the Trainers' Networks continue to maintain their links, the Forest School Association and Forest School Wales have few links, and the dates of the two annual conferences and AGM tend to both fall in the October half-term holiday, meaning that even if practitioners wished to attend both, they are forced to make a choice. Whilst the Foundation Phase curriculum explicitly supports Forest School as a preferred outdoor learning option, Forest School in Wales will continue to thrive. But the statutory school starting age is still the same as in the rest of Great Britain, leaving the future as vulnerable as in England and even in Scotland. Working together is important, both to make the case for Forest School across the UK and to support practitioners as they develop their careers. Thankfully, the Trainers' Network link ensures that the dialogue between the three mainland countries remains open.

GOING FORWARD

REFLECTIONS ON FOREST SCHOOL

The Forest School Wales website (www.forestschoolwales.org.uk/ysgol-goedwigfor est-school/forest-school-ethos-history/) includes a section on the ethos and history of Forest School in the same way that the Forest School Association (www.forest schoolassociation.org/full-principles-and-criteria-for-good-practice/) lists the criteria for good practice. It is possible to map the one against the other and to value their shared ideals as well as to reflect on why they are expressed differently. Is it due to the longer period in which the Foundation Phase has been the chief focus of the Welsh development of Forest School? Or are there other pedagogical and philo-sophical drivers? What would it take to make it desirable to the trustees of the two charities for the two organisations to work together more closely, particularly now that there are other Forest School associations willing to work together, such as Forest School Canada (www.forestschoolcanada.ca/)?

IDEAS FOR PRACTICE: WOOD SLICES (FIGURE 5.3)

- Small slices can be cut by the less experienced and smaller hands can make counters and buttons.
- Medium-sized slices can make name tags and necklaces.
- Using a bow saw with two handles enables a practitioner to guide a learner in the correct way to hold a saw and where to place their other hand.
- A safety glove on the non-sawing hand helps prevent accidents, but wearing one on the sawing hand can weaken the grip on the saw.
- It is wise to have a discrete area for such tool use to prevent risks from passers-by.
- An appropriately sized and notched log or saw-horse will help keep the log to be sawn steady and secure.
- The height of the sawing surface needs to relate to the height of the person sawing.
- Larger slices can be rubbed smooth to make small plates and bases for artwork.

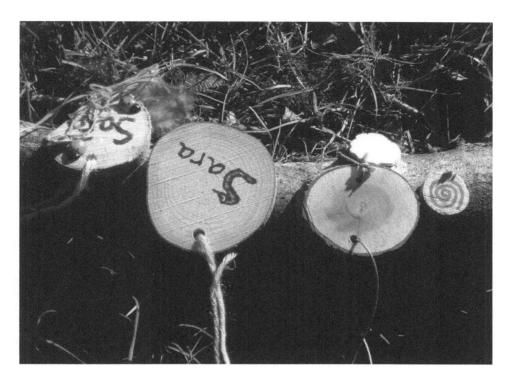

FIGURE 5.3 Wood Slices

FURTHER READING

- To understand the role of outdoor learning in general and Forest School in particular in the Welsh Foundation Phase, it is possible to download all the relevant documents at http://learning.gov.wales/resources/collections/foundation-phase?lang=en: 'Outdoor Learning: An Evaluation of Learning in the Outdoors' and 'Further Steps Outdoors' are under the resources tab, 'Foundation Phase Outdoor Learning Handbook' is under the guidance tab and the whole framework is under the curriculum tab.
- The Forestry Commission Wales commissioned a research project into the value of Forest School based on a Welsh site: see Hughes, F. & Jenner, L. (2006) *Pentre Forest School: An Evaluation of a Forest School Project*. Ruthin: Forestry Commission Wales. This report gives an insight into Welsh Forest School.
- Tim Gill has undertaken a literature review of the evidence of the benefits to children's development of being outdoors: see Gill, T. (2014) 'The benefits of children's engagement with nature: a systematic literature review', *Children, Youth and Environments*, 24(2): 10–34. This article offers a useful set of arguments in favour of all outdoor learning and play-based experiences.

6

Ireland

Only Northern Ireland is a part of the UK. The Republic of Ireland is a different independent country. However, as there are links between the Forest School community in the Republic of Ireland and in the UK, I am going to mention the developments there at the end of this chapter. But I will start with Northern Ireland and an overview of the curriculum as it relates to children between the ages of 3 and 5 years. I will then consider what Forest School could offer this age group in Northern Ireland in particular.

In Northern Ireland, children start school in September, at the beginning of the academic year, if they have reached the age of 4 by the previous 1 July, and so are aged between 4 years and 2 months and 5 years and 2 months on starting. In exceptional circumstances, this can be deferred, but that would be unusual. The first two years of schooling are called the foundation stage. In the whole of the Primary Curriculum document (Council for the Curriculum, Examinations and Assessment, 2007), which includes the foundation stage as well as Key Stages 1 and 2, the word 'outdoor' occurs four times and 'forest' not at all. Of those four occurrences, the first is in the section on mathematics where it states that movement through space can occur outside. The next two occurrences are in the section on physical development, once to explain that exuberant outdoor play is an excellent way to let off steam and once to exhort schools to provide daily physical activities either indoors or outside. The last occurrence is to state that children will have had more outdoor experiences in their preschool settings.

The Curricular Guidance for Pre-School Education 2014 (Council for the Curriculum, Examinations and Assessment, 2014) does mention 'outdoor' more often, some 13 times, but again there is no mention of 'forest'. The first occurrence of 'outdoor' is in the context of exhorting practitioners to *create* learning environments indoors and out (not discover or encounter), but it does then follow this with three more mentions that outdoor learning should be an integral part of the experience, is unique and should be frequent. The next seven occurrences are in the context of unpicking particular curriculum areas in turn, each of which can be explored 'indoors and outside' (in that order). When it comes to encouraging and monitoring progress, it is acknowledged that outdoor play 'can provide space and freedom that it would be difficult to find indoors. It has an important role in the emotional development of children', which is encouraging until the last mention which is that 'all outdoor space, whether large or small, should be defined for particular planned activities in order to maximise its use and ensure that children can play safely'. The 'Learning Outdoors in the Early Years' booklet (Bratton et al., 2009), published through the Council for the Curriculum, Examinations and Assessment, suggests ways to achieve these curriculum and safety goals within the nursery or preschool setting. On the last page, it includes a description of what Forest School might be, but without guidance for how or where to access such provision.

It appears that the research findings on the benefits of wilder outdoor play in general and Forest School in particular, which I have discussed previously (Knight, 2015), have made no impression on the Northern Ireland Government's Department of Education. The benefits to the learning and development of young children of learning to work in teams, to socialise, to communicate and to feel good about themselves are completely overlooked. And the word 'sustainability' does not occur at all in either of the two key documents considered so far. It is not surprising, therefore, to find that Forest School in Northern Ireland exists largely due to the efforts and leadership of one person (see Case Study 6.1).

CASE STUDY 6.1: BRIAN POOTS AND THE NIFSA

In the early noughties, Brian Poots consulted with the group that eventually formed the FSA for the whole of the UK. In the past, Brian had worked as a Senior Ecologist for Landlife and Conservation Volunteers Northern Ireland and as a Senior Woodland Officer for the Woodland Trust, and has been developing and delivering environmental education programmes for over thirty years, so his expertise was greatly valued. Since then, Brian has been responsible for setting up the Northern Ireland Forest School Association (NIFSA) and continues to work in the province to further the shared aims of the NIFSA and the umbrella FSA, as can be seen from his communication below. The NIFSA includes a map of members (nifsa.org.uk/find-a-forest-school-near-you/#).

Brian writes: 'I set up the Northern Ireland Forest School Association (NIFSA) in September 2008. It is a registered charity. We receive no core funding and exist by selling our services and securing grant aid. I am currently the only paid member of staff, although we have a group of around eight volunteers. I have developed a Level 3 Award in Forest School Leadership (6 credits) that is accredited by the Open College Network NI. This has now gone through the Qualification Curriculum Framework and so is on the Register of Recognised Qualifications in Northern Ireland.

I have worked with around 25 organisations, delivering the Level 3 Award for them. This is a 12-week programme working with a teacher or teachers and their class, one day a week. We usually walk to their local park for the activities. This is right across Northern Ireland. These have been mainly Primary Schools but recently there has been a big interest from Nursery Schools. I work with about 6–8 organisations per year, and I also deliver training to one of the Teacher Training Colleges in Belfast. NIFSA offer a complete package to organisations wanting training and development. We can source the funding to support the initiative, deliver the training and accreditation, we encourage organisations to stay in touch with NIFSA through the NIFSA Monthly Newsletter and registration on the NIFSA Nature Ranger Scheme (this is an annual certification scheme for those accredited Forest Schools, see nifsa.org.uk/nifsa-nature-ranger-scheme/).

There is definitely a growing interest in Forest Schools but in the current financial climate, and unfortunately the lack of interest by the Northern Ireland Assembly, you have to be creative to be able to support those organisations wanting to become a Forest School. In 2015, a new magazine in Northern Ireland called Freckle (www.frecklenorthernireland.org/) in the summer published a piece on the Forest School project outlining how it can benefit minority groups in disadavantaged areas. I also ran a cross-community project with Holy Family and Currie Primary Schools in 2015; a Protestant and a Catholic School using NIFSA Forest School every Thursday to bring the two communities together. I am working on another cross-community Forest School in 2016.'

What is remarkable is that Brian has achieved as much as he has. There is a specific Northern Ireland Level 3 leadership award available that is on the Register of Recognised Qualifications in Northern Ireland. There is a Northern Ireland Forest School Association (NIFSA), with a map of 16 registered and active Forest School groups in the province and a regular newsletter to share good news and ideas. There is a DVD on the website about Forest School in Northern Ireland that all can access. The NIFSA can and do raise funds and secure grants to support projects. As the website states: 'The whole experience excites and inspires the children and there is often plenty of laughing and fun to be had' (http://nifsa.org.uk/typical-day/).

What I find particularly inspiring is the work that Brian is doing with primary schools to bridge the sectarian divide, a source of historical violence and ongoing discord. Northern Ireland has different categories of school which speak to this discord. The controlled schools are those that were originally Protestant church schools and were transferred to state control in the first half of the 20th century, with four of the nine governors in each school being representatives from one or more of the three main Protestant churches. Although they are now theoretically open to those of any or no faith, the statutory role of the Protestant governors is still in place. In the academic year 2015/16, the enrolments in September at primary schools in this category numbered 368 (DENI, 2015: 4). Additionally, there were 64 enrolments in controlled nursery schools.

Then there are Catholic-managed schools supported by the Council for Catholic Maintained Schools, which includes representatives from the Department of Education NI plus Trustees recommended by the Catholic bishops in Northern Ireland, as well as teachers and parents. Again, these schools are theoretically open to children from any or no faith, but the teaching is done in accordance with Catholic traditions. In the academic year 2015/16, the enrolments in September at primary schools in this category numbered 374 (DENI, 2015: 4). There were 32 enrollments in Catholic maintained nursery schools. Of the 827 children enrolled in primary schools in that academic year, 742 of them were enrolled in potentially segregated school communities, some 89 per cent.

There were 43 enrolments in schools promoting integration, and 29 enrolments in 'other' primaries, plus 13 in preparatory schools. The 43 are in schools established by the Integrated Education Fund (IEF), set up in 1992 in response to parental demand for integrated education. The funds come from the European Union, the Nuffield Foundation and the Joseph Rowntree Charitable Trust as well as the Department of Education NI, with the aim of supporting new schools until they can gain full government funding. As can be seen from the statistics above, in 23 years the IEF has progressed to securing places for 5 per cent of the children enrolling in primary schools. The 29 'other' includes Irish-medium schools, called Gaelscoileanna, where children are taught most subjects through the medium of Gaeilge, the Irish language, established by the Education (Northern Ireland) Order 1998 and creating, along with the fee-paying children in preparatory schools, another potentially segregated section of the population. With only the identified 5 per cent of children enrolling in integrated school, it would seem that creating a truly integrated community in the province is a long way off, unless other ways can be found to bridge the divides.

Research, such as that by Davis and Waite in 2005, highlights the many benefits of Forest School to children aged 3–5 and explicitly mentions their developing sense of community (Davis & Waite, 2005: 19), their ability to articulate their thoughts and ideas (ibid.: 20) and their developing skills in expressing their own beliefs and values (ibid.: 21). This is to touch on a core aspect of Forest School that is only recently being openly discussed – the opportunity it offers for us to enter the spiritual domain that is a necessary feature of being human and one which is largely ignored in modern life. I argue that Forest School creates opportunities for connectivity between the space and time offered in Forest School sessions (Knight, 2016d), young children's natural creativity and their spiritual connection with their inner selves. The images in Figure 6.1 show how children can respond to a tree and some natural resources to express their feelings.

Wattchow and Brown encourage outdoor practitioners to recognise the power of a sensory engagement with place (2011: 196) as an 'active journey towards belonging. With belonging comes connection and the development of an ethic of care.' This seems to encapsulate Forest School experiences as I have observed them. Gray (2012) explores 'the Deweyian idea of experience and education' and considers the power of learning as a situated process, giving that power to outdoor learning experiences over the more Cartesian classroom-based learning, i.e. one based on the separation of mind and body that seems to be the norm in so many classrooms. Gray's idea of the body–environment interaction as a key to cognitive processes supports the observations of earlier researchers that children in Forest School settings acquire skills differently from the way in which they do in their classroom-based learning. The process is holistic and is located in the interaction between the children and the place and the children and each other, with the practitioners as sensitive facilitators of that process. Horning (2011: 56) describes using Forest School sessions to ease the transition of pupils from different primary schools into the same integrated high school class. If children from different schools can find ways to integrate in Forest School sessions and to express and explore their thoughts, ideas and beliefs, then hopefully they will go on to understand better how all the disparate communities in Northern Ireland can cohere into one.

The Republic of Ireland, which was fully constituted in 1948 from the Irish Free State, itself founded in 1922 as a result of the Anglo-Irish Treaty of 1921, is a member of the European Union and the Euro zone. It has many similarities with other European states, not least in that the compulsory school starting age is 6 years. However, children can be enrolled in primary school from the age of 4 and some 40 per cent of parents take up that opportunity. The Primary Curriculum dates from 1999 and is dual-language Gaeilge (Irish) and English (National Council for Curriculum and Assessment, 1999). The preschool years are covered by Síolta, the National Quality Framework for Early Childhood Education, published in 2006, and Aistear, the Early Childhood Curriculum Framework, published in 2009. As it is the latter two that cover the age range under discussion

FIGURE 6.1   Tree Face

and they are more recent documents, it is in them that I will look for links to Forest School. (The Aistear documents can be accessed at www.ncca.ie/ en/Curriculum_and_Assessment/Early_Childhood_and_Primary_Education/ Early_Childhood_Education/Framework_for_early_learning/ and the Síolta documents at www.dcya.gov.ie/docs/National_Quality_Framework_for_Early_ Childhood_Care_and_Educ/383.htm.)

In the Síolta guidance for infant classes, which cover that 40 per cent of children entering school before the compulsory age, there are frequent mentions of 'outdoors' and none of 'forest', just as in the Northern Ireland early years documents. However, there are differences in that on at least two occasions the indoor/outdoor reference is expressed as outdoor/indoor – a subtle change but indicative of attitude. And at point 2.5.1 (Centre for Early Childhood Development & Education, 2006: 22), practitioners are exhorted to provide and promote outdoor activities that challenge and provide safe risks (an interesting description). Aistear also has frequent mentions of 'outdoors', and in the guidelines for good practice encourages the idea of free-flow play between indoors and outdoors (National Council for Curriculum and Assessment, 2009: 55). Nowhere is there any mention of Forest School. However, Maynooth University in County Kildare contains the Froebel Department of Primary and Early Childhood Education, which promotes the Froebelian philosophy of child-centred, play-based practice and the importance of the outdoor environment. The department supports research into such subjects as play and exploring physical environments as mediums for teaching and learning within Aistear. And the *ChildLinks* magazine, published by Barnardos, the leading children's charity in Ireland, has included an issue on the importance of risk (Barnardos, 2011) and the importance of a socio-cultural pedagogy (ibid., 2008). These elements are all a part of Forest School practice, and so it is not surprising to find that Forest School is, indeed, beginning to flourish in Ireland.

In 2013, an article in the *Irish Times* described Forest School as alive and well in Ireland. Ranelagh School in Dublin and Nature School in County Mayo have had Forest School sessions running since then. Nature School hosts Level 3 training validated through the Open College Network West Midlands and received an Irish Forestry Award in 2015 that specifically mentioned its commitment to outdoor education. At least three major training groups from England have been active in delivering training in Ireland and there are 15 sites listed as actively involved in Forest School in some way or another on the Earth Force Education website (www.earthforce education.com/). Rather than one person engaged in the Promethean task of launching Forest School across the country, as in Northern Ireland, in the Republic of Ireland there would seem to be competition and enthusiasm to train and establish delivery sites for Forest School. And at the 2015 FSA conference, there was a delegate from Ranelagh School in Dublin, Ireland, who responded to my survey, indicating an interest in collaboration and cooperation for the future.

GOING FORWARD

REFLECTIONS ON FOREST SCHOOL

Some pedagogical issues are being mentioned that are worthy of deeper consideration and this is reflected in the recommended reading for this chapter. To prepare for this, practitioners working with children under 7 years old could consider how they would evidence that their practice is democratic and that the voice of the child is heard. Ask yourselves the following questions: Can you demonstrate that your Forest School sessions are child-centred, child-led and play-based? Do you facilitate the children's needs for awe and wonder, creativity and self-expression? How would a visitor know this? Are there challenges and risks to overcome and learn from in your settings?

IDEAS FOR PRACTICE: MUD FACES

Figure 6.1 is an illustration of a mud face decorated with found objects. This was done by primary-aged children. Figure 6.2 shows younger children engaged in making mud faces. I have also done this activity with adults from undergraduate to doctoral colleagues. It is just one of those activities that can be as meaningful and deep as the people engaging with it choose to make it. And its artistic merit is irrelevant. It is a form of self-expression or a way of finding the inner spirit of a tree or all stages in between:

- Make a patch of mud with water, earth and a stirring device.
- If required, collect this in an old bucket or saucepan.
- Scrape together a hand-sized blob – use an old spoon or just fingers.
- Mould it in your hand.
- Stick it to the tree of your choice.
- Add more mud if required.
- Shape it as feels appropriate to the relationship between you and the tree.
- Add found objects such as feathers, seed heads and leaves.
- Stand back and admire your creation.

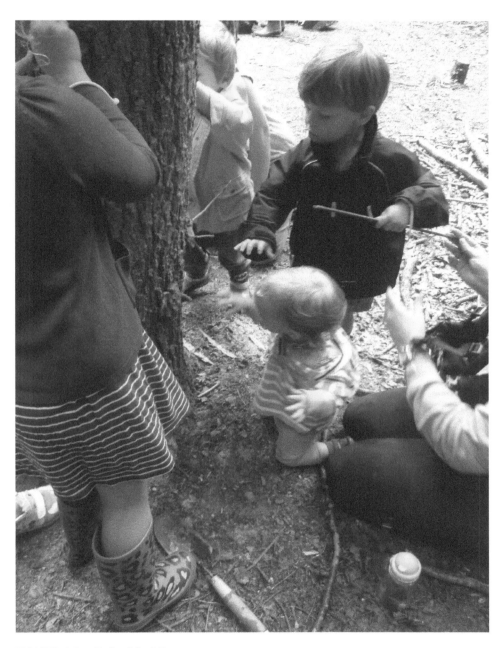

FIGURE 6.2   Baby Mud Faces

FURTHER READING

- The ideas that Froebel had about kindergarten are very relevant to Forest School. Read about them in *Early Childhood Practice: Froebel Today*, written by Tina Bruce in 2012, or visit an English-language online resource about Friedrich Froebel, creator of the kindergarten (www.froebelweb.org/), for an alternative perspective.
- Theorists more relevant to the primary years and beyond are explored in *Understanding and Using Educational Theories* by Aubrey and Riley (2015). There are useful chapters on Dewey (mentioned in this chapter) and Claxton (mentioned in a previous chapter).
- Pedagogical ideas about the importance of 'place' have gained much ground in outdoor education, moving in from the discipline of Social Geography. I have mentioned Wattchow and Brown's (2011) *A Pedagogy of Place*, based in Australia and New Zealand but relevant to developing a Forest School pedagogy.

7

England

Forest School was developed in England in 1994 initially for nursery-aged children, and yet 20 years later the 2014 Early Years Foundation Stage barely mentions outdoor provision, other than to say that 'activities should take place outdoors on a daily basis' (Dept for Education, 2014a: 28). In spite of this, there are many thousands of nurseries, reception classes and pre-schools that offer Forest School to their 3–5-year-olds. This tension between the politics of the statutory and funded provision and what practitioners believe to be in the best interests of the developing child is highlighted by the increasingly enthusiastic reactions to Forest School of Ofsted inspectors. This chapter will explore the ways in which national and local early years policies have seesawed between support for and indifference to outdoor provision in general and Forest School in particular, and evaluate the impact this has had on the spread of Forest School in England for this age group. Alongside this, the impact made by different individuals at certain points in this story will be explored and evaluated.

The role of the Forest Education Initiative (FEI), part of the Forestry Commission, was not as central as in Wales and Scotland, largely because the percentage of land owned by the Commission is so much less. However, the Forest School coordinator for England, Susannah Podmore, was instrumental in supporting early funding bids to the Woodland Improvement Grant scheme and was closely involved with the setting up of the Forest School Association. Many local groups are still based on the old FEI cluster groups.

The compulsory school starting age in England is the beginning of the term following a child's fifth birthday (Dept for Education, 2014b), as it has been since 1870. However, the Schools Admissions Code requires local authorities to provide school places in the September following children's fourth birthday and this has become the normal school starting age. As the Early Years Foundation Stage curriculum applies to children between 3 and 5 years, reception classes in schools are required to follow that, rather than Key Stage 1 of the Primary Curriculum. And all private, voluntary and state early years provision is required to follow the EYFS if it is to be registered to offer state-funded places. It is therefore to that curriculum that this chapter will refer.

The Early Years Foundation Stage (EYFS) was launched in 2006 into a vibrant and diverse sector alive with research and keen to promote play-based learning (Male & Palaiologou, 2016). The political pressure from governments from the 1990s onwards on a workforce strongly influenced by Froebel, Dewey, Isaacs et al. to increasingly focus on developing literacy in the preschool years, rather than to follow the holistic approach favoured by early years experts, had helped the development of counter-movements such as Forest School, which are designed to provide children with the experiences that most practitioners felt were more appropriate. In the years between the formation of the Early Years Development and Childcare Partnerships in 2001 and the introduction of the EYFS in 2006, a generation of early years advisors had trained as Forest School practitioners and were using Forest School sessions to support families at risk, particularly once Children's Centres were established in 2006 (Partridge & Taylor, 2011). Although the 2006 EYFS did contain more formal measures of academic progress than many early years experts felt were appropriate, it did also contain a requirement that all children should play outside every day, which has affected the environments and policies in day nurseries, particularly those in inner cities, and has given those settings interested in Forest School some support to continue. This requirement has survived the 2012 and 2014 revisions when other guidance promoting practices such as free-flow play and child-initiated activities (DCSF, 2008: 7) have disappeared.

What also did not survive the change of political leadership from 2010 was the level and nature of the support that Forest School was receiving from the local authorities via the early years advisors. This was not because the advisors themselves had lost their enthusiasm, as can be seen in the case studies. But cuts in funding have required local authorities to reduce staff numbers and have usually additionally placed a duty on those staff left in post to recover the costs for their work wherever possible. I have taken a line across the middle of England to gather the case studies that show the impact

FIGURE 7.1   Map of English Counties

of the changes on the support for Forest School, starting in Norfolk (Case Study 7.1) and crossing to Shropshire (Case Study 7.4) via Cambridgeshire (Case Study 7.2) and Oxfordshire (Case Study 7.3). Apologies to the counties that I have leapfrogged over, some of which will be mentioned elsewhere, but similar pictures can be inferred from the studies included.

CASE STUDY 7.1: FOREST SCHOOL IN NORFOLK – AN EVOLVING SITUATION

Written by Sue Falch-Lovesey (Head of Environmental and Outdoor Learning, Norfolk County Council) and Louise Ambrose (Birchwood Learning, Norfolk), with edits by Sara Knight.

Norfolk was comparatively quick off the mark in its early explorations of Forest School, given that it is an easterly county and Forest School had begun in the West of England, with Norfolk County Council (NCC) involved in researching and training advisors and teachers in the early noughties. Meanwhile, new international links between Norfolk and Norwegian schools in Trondheim further fired the imagination and stimulated developments. These early links were set up by NCC's School Organisation Team and gave officers and teachers an opportunity to seek out and be inspired by practice in other countries. This partnership has grown and there are deep links with Trondheim and Sør Trondelag County, with over 20 Norwegian Sixth Form students now studying in Norfolk schools each year.

A small pilot programme in 2005, based at Houghton Hall (thanks to Lord Chomondeley) and in partnership with a local primary school, was quickly followed by Norfolk-based Level 1 and Level 3 training programmes backed by NCC. From the earliest development of Forest Schools in Norfolk, partnership work has been key to building capacity. Over 10 years of NCC-funded coordination, Forest School has grown slowly, steadily and sustainably. The early days of training in the county were subsidised by grants that NCC received from the Forestry Commission Woodland Improvement Grant Scheme. The early years team within NCC also funded a number of places for early years practitioners in certain districts. The known qualified Level 3 practitioners total approximately 200, whilst there are roughly 50 Level 2s and over 650 Level 1s. There is, however, no way of accurately determining how many of these practitioners are actively involved with running Forest School.

From 2015, as the Forest School Association (FSA) Norfolk local group has grown and strengthened, Norfolk County Council has stepped back from direct coordination and training – encouraging the networks to take up any training demand and support requirements. Demand for Forest School, however, continues and the networks of practitioners are strong. These networks could be tapped into in the future by partners (including the County Council), should there be a need, and will be for more coordinated development of specific provision. NCC has undertaken evaluations of case studies which are on the FSA Norfolk website (http://fsanorfolk.wix.com/fsan#!case-studies/l7iba) and which contribute to the researched evidence of the benefits of Forest School.

Thanks to the commitment and energy of a highly motivated group of Level 3 practitioners, Forest School continues to evolve steadily, naturally and in response to the needs of the establishments that see the immense benefits for their youngest children. Forest School in Norfolk has possibly not yet reached its full potential, but it is well positioned to do so, and, though it is not dependent on the financial backing of a local authority, there is still a willingness and enthusiasm by all to work in collaboration for the good of Norfolk children.

CASE STUDY 7.2: CAMBRIDGESHIRE

At the time of writing Allison Box is the Forest School Advisor on the Early Years Advisory team at Cambridgeshire County Council. She trained over six years ago and since then has supported the development of Forest School across Cambridgeshire through county events and individual support until the majority of preschool settings and primary schools (including reception classes) can access sessions or run them themselves. The academic year 2013/14 saw her role become reliant on generating an income from the support she offers and as a training facilitator. Despite working only half of her week in this role, Allison continues to run an annual conference in the county, Forest School Network twilight and evening sessions and CPD courses. These are well-attended full-cost-recovery events. She liaises with local outdoor interest groups such as Cambridge Curiosity and Imagination (CCI) (www.cambridgecandi.org.uk/) and Natural Cambridgeshire. The latter incorporates the Naturally Healthy initiative, aiming to encourage health services to prescribe restorative experiences within the natural environment as an alternative/in addition to medication. Allison also liaises with the national FSA.

In 2012, she undertook a research project to compare Early Years Foundation Stage Profile data between children in Cambridgeshire who had participated in Forest School (supported by CCI) and children in Cambridgeshire who had not, and found a clear improvement in the communication skills of the FS group (see Figure 7.2.i).

In 2014, Allison supported a further research project to investigate the impact of Forest School on the self-esteem of Pupil Premium Funded (PPF) primary-aged children (the researcher involved was Debbie Squire, the Forest School leader at Waterbeach Primary School). Findings demonstrated improvement in self-esteem immediately following a term of Forest School sessions and also 8 weeks after (see Figures 7.2.ii and 7.2.iii). Furthermore, the impact was seen by teachers back in the classroom who observed improvements in the children's confidence when engaging with their academic work. The use of PPF (both in schools and early years settings) to fund FS projects is becoming more commonplace throughout Cambridgeshire. This innovative use of funding to accelerate children's achievements is contributing to Allison's role remaining self-sustaining.

Allison's commitment to Forest School is keeping the impetus for Forest School going in early years settings and in primary education. Her research data will add to the growing body of evidence supporting the efficacy of Forest School in the Foundation Stage and beyond.

(Continued)

(Continued)

7.2.i Comparison of EYFSP 2012 data for cohort attending/not attending weekly woodland learning sessions who were working securely within Communication, Language and Literacy (Language for Communication and Thinking; Reading Early Learning Goals).

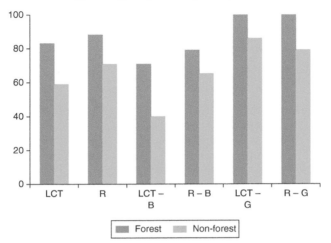

LCT: Language for Communication and Thinking, R: Reading,
LCT-B: Language for Communication and Thinking Boys, R-B: Reading Boys,
LCT-G: Language for Communication and Thinking Girls, R-G: Reading Girls.

7.2.ii Rosenberg Self-esteem Scale   7.2.iii Coopersmith Self-Esteem Inventory

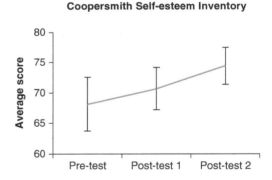

FIGURE 7.2   Cambridge Research Data

Reading the case studies, the continuing enthusiasm and commitment at all levels is apparent. What is interesting is the changing nature of the relationship. In Case Study 7.1, Norfolk County Council initially took a strong lead, working with the Green Light Trust from their base in Suffolk to train leaders who would then be able to lead training themselves. As the number of practitioners has grown and the level of county council funding has shrunk, those committed trainers have gone on to encourage the formation of a strong local Forest School Association (FSA) group, which organises a range of meetings and courses and collects evaluated case studies on its website as evidence of the benefits of Forest School. The county council has seen its 'child' grow up and become a partner for the future.

In Cambridgeshire, Case Study 7.2, the early years team members were always facilitators rather than providers. When the Forest School movement in the county was just beginning, they ran highly subsidised events to encourage practitioners to get involved. Now that most early years settings have encountered Forest School in one way or another, the funding cuts have been less critical than they could have been and full-cost-recovery training events still attract a full attendance. The Cambridgeshire FSA conferences usually welcome over a hundred early years professionals and teachers. The facilitator role continues, but with the Forest School community as customers and with the Forest School advisor supporting research into the measurable benefits of Forest School.

CASE STUDY 7.3: OXFORDSHIRE

Oxfordshire was one of the first counties to embrace Forest School, particularly for the 3–5-year-old age group. The county's outdoor centre at Hill End, just west of Oxford city, has been a focus for Forest School activity, particularly when Jenny Doyle was appointed as the Forest School coordinator in the early noughties. Jenny had been important as one of the founders of the FSA and had previously done ground-breaking work in Worcestershire, based at the Bishop's Wood Environmental Centre with Jon Cree. Since her retirement, her post has been ably filled by Karen Cahill as the Forest School coordinator and Sarah Lawful as the lead trainer, who writes:

'Hill End Centre has had an important role in Oxfordshire's Forest School journey, hosting training for over 16 years. Since 2010 our beautiful 64 acre site has been the permanent home of Oxfordshire Forest School Service, providing a rich variety of woodland, meadow and stream habitats for Forest School and Outdoor Learning training. We work with educators, children's centres, child minders offering Forest School taster days to share the exciting opportunities Forest School offers children, young people and families alongside a regular programme of training.

The main focus of our work has been training and supporting teachers and practitioners to be Forest School Leaders and Assistants. Our expertise is also drawn on by Advisory Teachers and early years settings to support the development of their outdoor areas and develop their practice to meet the priorities of the Children and Young People's Plan 2015–2018 (Oxfordshire Children's Trust, 2015).

(Continued)

(Continued)

Every Tuesday in term time we offer Forest Tots sessions. These sessions work with families, introducing them to child led natural play. Hill End staff welcome carers and their toddlers and provide simple resources, e.g. ropes, buckets, sand-pit toys and a mud kitchen, encouraging them to explore, following the children's lead. Through conversation and example, we show parents how to trust and enable their children to manage risk. The sessions are often inspired by the seasons and the weather. Waterproof suits are available for children who quickly build confidence, relishing the mud kitchen, puddles and grassy hills to roll down. Seasonal themed sessions with more adult initiated activities are planned every few weeks, such as Apple Day, Mud Day, Pancake Day or National Storytelling Week. We use fire with families to show them the possibilities of cooking together but often just sit and enjoy the multi-sensory experience.

There is now a core of regular attendees who brave all weathers. A pop-up café ensures that physical needs are met, proving especially popular in the winter months. From experience, we know that summer days will see more families coming, often settling down to picnics towards the end of each session, reluctant to leave'.

CASE STUDY 7.4: SHROPSHIRE

Alice Savery was appointed as Forest School Development Officer in January 2006. This was as a part of the Education Improvement Service at Shropshire Council, recognising the value of Forest School sessions in improving children's educational performance. Shropshire Council had been nurturing the Forest School initiative in the county since 2002 when a steering group formed, comprised of representatives from the former Shropshire County Council's Early Years and Childcare team, local woodland owners and environmental educators. This group became registered as a Forest Education Initiative (FEI) cluster group in 2003. The Shropshire Early Years Development Childcare Partnership (EYDCP) soon provided funding for a two-year pilot project. This involved establishing an exemplar Shropshire County Council Forest School site, to the south of Shrewsbury, with a small team delivering Forest School sessions to local schools and settings. The team consisted of a part-time Forest School coordinator, with two Forest School leaders to deliver sessions at the exemplar site. In 2006, the coordinator post increased in hours and changed to become that of Forest School Development Officer. From 2008 to 2015, the post was full time, coordinating a team of Forest School leaders delivering Forest School sessions at four exemplar woodland sites in Shropshire and on school grounds. In September 2015, the role was reduced to three days a week but Alice continues to promote Forest School in Shropshire, to organise and deliver Forest School training and CPD courses, and to run Forest School sessions with a range of age groups.

Alice also continues to support the many Forest School practitioners in Shropshire, holding regular network meetings. She chaired the Shropshire and Telford & Wrekin FEI Cluster Group for many years, which had representatives from a diverse group of organisations including the Shropshire Wildlife Trust, the Green Wood Centre, the Shropshire Hills Discovery Centre, the Wyre Forest Discovery Centre, the South Shropshire AONB and the North Shropshire Countryside Unit. Although this cluster has faded in recent years, through the annual Forest School Shropshire conference links are maintained with those local and national organisations. In 2015, Alice was responsible for organising the FSA national conference in the county, at Condover Hall.

Shropshire Council continues to support the exemplar Forest School woodland sites which are located as follows:

- south of Shrewsbury, near Condover
- north of Shrewsbury, near Hadnall
- in the south of the county, near Ludlow
- in the Oswestry area, near West Felton.

These are sites staffed by the Forest School team, employed by the council. Local schools and settings can access sessions at these sites throughout the academic year. The idea is that the school or early years setting will access Forest School sessions for the whole academic year. However, to enable other groups to access it, sessions are often broken down into visits for the whole or half of a term. This is often the starting point, with training then becoming the sustainable option, enabling staff from the settings to then lead sessions themselves. The majority of primary schools and early years settings in Shropshire now have staff who are Forest School leader-trained. They deliver Forest School sessions regularly in their own school grounds. With the growing number of practitioners in Shropshire and therefore a growing number of children accessing the approach, Alice has developed an interest in case studies and research in Forest School with a paper accepted for publication in *Education 3–13* in 2016 (Savery et al., 2016).

As stated in Case Study 7.3, Oxfordshire was one of the first counties involved in Forest School as it spread east from Somerset. Like Norfolk, the advisors developed FS training at their centre at Hill End as well as offering the delivery of sessions. This continues and still feeds into the work of the county advisors but is no longer subsidised. What has expanded is the delivery of a range of activities at Hill End, including 'Forest Tots', described in the case study. This diversification is into a growth area for Forest School – that of working with parents and young children – as we shall see in Chapter 14.

Shropshire County (Case Study 7.4) established a Forest School Development Officer in 2002, at a time when the FEI cluster groups were popular, so here was a county where the facilitation of communication between interested parties was paramount, a role that continues. In parallel, the county continues in 2016 to subsidise the provision of sessions in four sites in the county, which is keeping the level of FS provision high in early years settings and primary schools. The development officer, despite having her hours reduced, is also able to contribute to the growing body of research supporting the efficacy of Forest School in these age groups.

In the case studies, we have four different county models with differing levels of involvement in the delivery of Forest School in settings. Whether initially primarily 'parenting', in partnership or with ownership of delivery, cuts have required levels of reinvention which, in most instances, seem to be energising key practitioners to ensure there is a continuing Forest School provision. For 3–5-year-olds in England, it is still expanding despite the financial cuts being experienced by the state sector. This is because the theoretical underpinnings of Forest School are in synergy with those of the early years sector, as the endeavours of leaders to generate evidence of the benefits of Forest School demonstrate. As we will see in the next chapter, freely chosen play and intrinsic motivation are as fundamental to good Forest School practice as they are to quality early years provision. Laying down habits of fresh air and exercise are common to both, as are developing those caring attitudes that are fundamental to developing a commitment to sustainability.

What is interesting is the way in which Ofsted, the inspection regime in England, has recognised the value of Forest School, as can be seen in Case Study 7.5. Ofsted is the Office for Standards in Education, Children's Services and Skills. It is responsible for the inspection and regulation of services that care for children and young people, and services providing education and skills for learners of all ages. Following an inspection, it rates a school or setting on a four-point scale. Receiving one of the highest two grades, Outstanding or Good, may mean that the setting will not be re-inspected for five years. 'Requires Improvement' and 'Inadequate' will generate further visits, and the latter rating may generate intensive interactions with the local authorities under the 'Special Measures' scheme. Ultimately, the setting may end up being closed. Naturally, this generates close attention to Ofsted's views, and the positive comments made about Forest School sessions have given practitioners considerable encouragement.

CASE STUDY 7.5: OFSTED'S REACTIONS TO FOREST SCHOOL

On its website, Ofsted gives examples of good practice in early years to encourage others and one such is 'Using a forest environment for pre-school children', which includes the following extract:

Fleetwood's Charity Pre-school Group uses the forest school environment to provide a thrilling and inspiring environment for children to explore and take risks. Children thrive in this inclusive, exciting and stimulating setting, because practitioners focus their attention upon their unique and individual needs. They are healthy and safe and develop superb skills for the future. (Ofsted, 2012)

Other examples of citations of Forest School in Ofsted reports include:

1. Marsden Park Forest School, Marsden Hall, Lancashire, was rated 'Good' in 2013 by Ofsted: 'The leaders of the forest school have a strong commitment and enthusiasm to develop the setting further. This, and the support received from nursery and children's centre teams, means that they have a very good capacity for improvement.'
2. Mill View Primary School, Cheshire, was rated in 2013 an 'Outstanding school' with 'exciting Forest School provision'.
3. Oakwood House, Huddersfield received an Outstanding rating in 2013: 'Oakwood House Nursery and Forest School is surrounded by wooded gardens providing plenty of scope for the highest quality outdoor play and learning.'
4. Reflections Nursery, Worthing, was graded 'Outstanding' by Ofsted in 2014. Inspectors noted that Reflections provides some unique opportunities for children, including a Forest School programme taking children into local woodland two days a week.
5. Sandy Lane Nursery and Forest School, Cheshire, received an 'Outstanding' rating by Ofsted in 2012: 'The school continues to be outstanding and has improved since the previous inspection by becoming a Forest school with its own woodland next to the outdoor play area.'
6. Seething and Mundham, Norfolk, was graded 'Good' by Ofsted in 2014: 'The school teaches a wide range of interesting subjects ... these are enhanced by a strong "Forest School" programme ... [which] contribute[s] to pupils' strong spiritual, moral, social and cultural development.'

All quotations are taken from Ofsted reports available online and represent a wide geographical coverage. This means that more than one inspection team is recognising the value of Forest School.

Alongside the support from Ofsted, the enthusiasm of practitioners and the growing body of research data, the media regularly run stories that wax lyrical about children lighting fires and learning life skills at Forest School (for example, *The Guardian*, 13 May and 9 December 2014, 21 April 2015; *The Telegraph*, 13 June 2014, 8 December 2015; *The Times*, July 2011). The English Department for Education 2014 curriculum has no mention of Forest School, no mention of outdoor education until Key Stage 2 when it occurs once in the PE syllabus, and no mention of sustainability in the early years or primary curriculum at all. Thankfully, there are enthusiastic practitioners in every county.

GOING FORWARD

REFLECTIONS ON FOREST SCHOOL

Practitioners will note that the key to growth and sustainability is partnership. Whether this is with landowners who allow Forest School sessions to take place on their property, with practitioners in cluster groups and through FSA membership, or with local authorities and organisations hosting training and conferences, Forest School grows through the shared enthusiasms of committed people. Reflect on this in different ways:

1   Humans are a social species and language is a key tool. Forest School encourages the development of communication but also needs it in order to flourish. How and where does this happen best?
2   The communications described in this chapter are largely bottom-up, with the practitioners creating the partnerships. There is little top-down policy to support Forest School. Does that matter? If there should be, what form should it take?
3   Why does Forest School create communicative partnerships? Is it intrinsic to practitioners?

IDEAS FOR PRACTICE: FIRE LIGHTING

The FSA website states that 'a successful safe camp fire can be a fabulous integral feature of your Forest School' (FSA, 2015b). There is something about fire that is so instinctively attractive that it is incumbent on practitioners not only to provide opportunities to create fires but also to teach children how to manage fire. Not to do so invites them to take unmanaged risks.

Whether fires are small, as in Figure 7.3 where children are preparing to take the one-strike challenge, or large, as in Figure 7.4 where a kettle is being readied for hot drinks, a fire needs to be attended to and managed. Some landowners do not allow fires to be lit on the ground, but this is not a barrier. Fires can be lit in a range of ways above the ground. The Scouts fact sheet describes an alter fire (Scout Association, 2013), and most DIY stores sell fire bowls. Some landowners do not allow fires to be lit at all. Their wishes do need to be respected but demonstrating the operation of a storm kettle can allay some fears. The FS Level 3 training includes instruction on safe distances for seating and how to move around a fire area as well as different ways to light fires, as do many bushcraft courses. Once confident that you can keep your group safe enough, it is incumbent on practitioners to light fires to create the central focal point for the group.

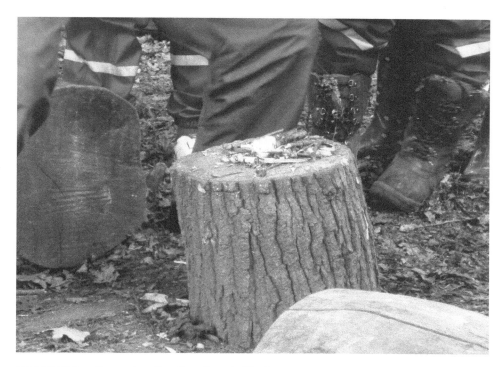

FIGURE 7.3   Preparing the One Spark Challenge

FIGURE 7.4   Tea Over a Camp Fire

FURTHER READING

- For an excellent description of the development of the modern early years education system in England, read Male, T. & Palaiologou, I. (2016) 'Historical developments in policy for early years education and care', in Palaiologou, I. (ed.) *The Early Years Foundation Stage*. London: Sage.
- Ofsted publishes exemplars to encourage settings to improve their practice. It is interesting to read the one that describes a Forest School, not least to see what features it focuses on. See Ofsted (2012) *Using a Forest Environment for Pre-school Children*. London: Ofsted.
- The Shropshire Forest School Development Officer has recently written a paper with colleagues based on research they have done in the county (Savery et al., 2016). This demonstrates one way in which councils can continue to support the development of Forest School.
- I recently considered the importance of Forest School as an holistic approach to learning: see Knight, S. (2016b) 'Forest school: a model for learning holistically and outdoors', in Lees, H.E. & Noddings, N. (eds) *The Palgrave International Handbook of Alternative Education*. London: Palgrave Macmillan.

Part 3

Forest School at Primary School

8

State Schools Compared

In England, education relating to sustainability and climate change was removed from the state curriculum for the under-14s in the 2013 amendments. However, sustainability and environmental issues are still at the heart of most school mission statements. Curiously, it is possible to be part of the Sustainable Schools Alliance (http://se-ed.co.uk/edu/sustainable-schools/sustainable-schools-alliance/) or to be registered as an Eco-school (www.eco-schools.org.uk/) without going outdoors at all. Conversely, it is possible to be neither of the above, and have pupils who learn outside and who are committed to caring about their environment. This invites questions about how people in general and young children in particular learn, learn about the environment, and learn to care about the environment. This chapter will begin to review the pedagogy of Forest School to reflect on its methodologies and some of the desired outcomes for children of primary school age.

CASE STUDY 8.1: HARTEST CEVC PRIMARY SCHOOL

Hartest Church of England Voluntary Controlled (CEVC) School is a small rural primary school in Suffolk. It may be significant that at Hartest the classes are named after trees which grow in the school grounds, indicating an ethos that is grounded in its environment:

(Continued)

FIGURE 8.1 Hartest Forest Scho

- Oak: Foundation – Reception
- Hazel: KS1 Years 1 and 2
- Willow: Lower KS2 Years 3 and 4
- Elder: Upper KS2 Years 5 and 6

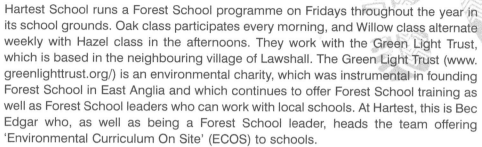

Hartest School runs a Forest School programme on Fridays throughout the year in its school grounds. Oak class participates every morning, and Willow class alternate weekly with Hazel class in the afternoons. They work with the Green Light Trust, which is based in the neighbouring village of Lawshall. The Green Light Trust (www.greenlighttrust.org/) is an environmental charity, which was instrumental in founding Forest School in East Anglia and which continues to offer Forest School training as well as Forest School leaders who can work with local schools. At Hartest, this is Bec Edgar who, as well as being a Forest School leader, heads the team offering 'Environmental Curriculum On Site' (ECOS) to schools.

For the Forest School sessions, the school uses a wooded piece of the school grounds that is separate from the rest, creating a special area for the unique ethos of Forest School. There, Bec can light a fire and facilitate activities. She uses the 'sit spot' technique for developing mindfulness with the reception children, and is able to follow their interests and respond to the changes in the environment with them. The older children are more interested in exploring activities that link into their class-based curriculum themes, but Bec finds that Forest School gives them the time and space to consolidate their ideas in ways not open to them in the classroom.

The case studies in this chapter relate to Forest School sessions for children at primary schools in different parts of the UK. As we have seen, Forest School for children in the Foundation Stage/Phase is becoming more readily available and the school in Case Study 8.1 follows this trend by offering sessions to the children in their reception year for a full morning a week for the whole year. The parents can access information about the sessions provided by the Green Light Trust on the school website and the emphasis is on the personal development that will come from them, the outcomes identified in the early research already cited (Borradaile, 2006; Davis & Waite, 2005; Hughes & Jenner, 2006; Knight, 2013; O'Brien & Murray, 2007). When it comes to the older children, in Years 1 to 4 they can participate in sessions on alternate Friday afternoons but the emphasis is on encouraging them to consolidate their in-class topic work through play. The school has appreciated the benefits of Forest School to help children to develop 'the mental, emotional and social resources to enjoy challenge and cope well with uncertainty and complexity' (Claxton et al., 2011: 2). I cite this text as I have agreed with colleagues that Claxton's ideas about 'Building Learning Power', as he calls it, relate well to the outcomes from Forest School sessions. What the teachers at Hartest have not yet grasped is the usefulness of Forest School to older primary-aged children. To do this, we need to examine the pedagogy more closely. But first let us consider Case Study 8.2.

CASE STUDY 8.2: WOOTTON PRIMARY SCHOOL

Wootton Community Primary School is one of over forty primary schools on the Isle of Wight. The village it serves was founded around the bridge over Wootton Creek and was first recorded in 1086. The school has an onsite nursery and a thriving holiday and afterschool provision. The name Wootton may be a corruption of Woodtown, meaning a clearing in a forest, so it is appropriate that the reception class have been sharing Forest School sessions on a Friday in a small clump of trees in the school grounds. Whilst there is a Forestry Commission woodland nearby, Firestone Copse, the school has not as yet negotiated an off-site location for their reception class sessions.

These are run by Geoff Mason, the director of Wood Learn Forest School (http://www.forestschooliow.co.uk/home), which runs sessions with different age groups all over the island. Geoff is a director of the Forest School Association, a qualified Forest School Practitioner, has the Bushcraft certificate for Practitioners, was the first qualified Beach School Practitioner on the Isle of Wight and now trains adults in this qualification. He brings 'Forest School in a van' to the school, setting up in the clump of trees with appropriate resources before supporting the children in their explorations of and interactions with the materials and each other. Whilst acknowledging that this is not his preferred way to deliver Forest School, he does believe that it provides many of the benefits of Forest School and is 'better than nothing', in that it is something, and something carefully thought out with the play-based child-led ethos of Forest School firmly at its roots.

In addition to the reception class session, Geoff also runs a ten-week block of Beach School sessions, which are funded through the Pupil Premium. This is additional funding for publicly funded schools in England to raise the attainment of disadvantaged pupils and close the gap between them and their peers. Most of the amount paid to schools is calculated on the basis of the numbers of children who are eligible for free school meals, an eligibility based on household income. The schools receiving this money can spend it in any way that they deem fit for the purpose, and in the case of Wootton School a proportion goes to pay for Beach School sessions, which, like Forest School sessions, are designed to raise the communication skills, confidence and self-esteem of a small group of children before they move on to secondary school.

Wootton School on the Isle of Wight, like Hartest and many others, appreciates the benefits of Forest School sessions for its youngest children, but is reluctant to commit scarce resources to funding transport costs for even these children. However, when it comes to supporting children entitled to the pupil premium, the school can see the purpose in investing the funds it has been given for these children into providing Forest or Beach School sessions. The skills that have been identified as measured outcomes in most of the published research to date are the very ones that could lift the educational outcomes for children who may be most at risk of failing at school. However, some schools are using Forest School in wider ways.

Clare Lamb, head teacher at All Saints Primary School in Suffolk and herself a Level 3 practitioner, has already described her whole-school approach to Forest School and all forms of outdoor learning (Lamb, 2011). In 2010, Ofsted awarded the school an 'Outstanding' grade, mentioning Forest School and noting that 'pupils' spiritual, moral, social and cultural development is outstanding' (Ofsted, in 2010, cited on school website). The school is now a National Support School with Clare as a National Leader of Education. She speaks of Forest School developing in children 'a sense of awe and wonder about the world around them, thus promoting deeper thinking and questioning skills to promote deeper understanding, the ability to be curious and explore and the desire to investigate and experiment' (Lamb, 2011: 37). She says that the holistic nature of the integrated curriculum enables children to see the purpose of learning and to apply subjects in context, making clear links between subjects and concepts (ibid.: 40).

Batheaston School in Bath has taken a similar approach, using Forest School plus other outdoor learning environments to provide a 'curriculum for all children [that] is innovative, creative and provides wide opportunities and real life experiences' (school website). In July 2013, this school was also designated as a National Support School with the head teacher, Sarah Weber, becoming a National Leader of Education. The practitioner who leads the Forest School experiences at the school, Julia Butler, undertook research on the outcomes of the Forest School sessions in the academic year 2014/15. Through observing children, interviewing parents and interrogating school records, the findings justify the whole-school approach. Not only did the research capture the expected outcome – that the 'experience supports key skills of independence, resourcefulness, resilience and communication' – but it also noted that this effect continues to build and develop over the time the children attend the school, with children sharing experiences across age and friendship groups. This study is unpublished but the school is happy to discuss the findings.

The differences in approaches to the usefulness of Forest School between the first two and the second two schools points to what Leather correctly describes as 'a theoretical and philosophical base (that) needs better articulating' (Leather, 2012). The benefits and theoretical underpinnings of Forest School are not clearly articulated enough for all head teachers to recognise their value. Like Leather, I do not claim to have the definitive answer to that need but I am prepared to contribute to the debate within the remaining chapters of this book. Figure 8.2 is my attempt at putting the key elements

Bushcraft

Biophilia

Sustainability

Mindfulness

Pedagogy of place

Pedagogy of time

Social Constructivist paradigm

Early years

Friluftsliv

Forest Education

Outdoor Ed

Play, freely chosen intrinsically motivated

FIGURE 8.2   Forest School Pedagogy

into a diagrammatic form. The tree represents Forest School. This is in itself problematic as different iterations of the event can look quite unalike and so to claim one diagram as adequate to describe all Forest School opportunities may be optimistic. However, whether the Forest School sessions are for 4-year-olds, 14-year-olds or 40-year-olds, they grow from the same earth, have the same basic premise and use the same branches of knowledge, albeit to varying degrees.

Consider the earth from which Forest School has grown. Previous chapters have acknowledged the debt owed to the Forestry Commission's Forest Education initiative, so this can be acknowledged as a part of that earth.

In addition, it has been noted that Forest School started as an early years initiative, and it is worth spending time considering two theoreticians influential in that field, namely Piaget and Vygotsky. O'Brien (2009), Leather (2012) and Harris (2015) all identify the constructivist and social constructivist nature of Forest School. The former descriptor can be applied to Piaget's ideas about how children construct knowledge from their direct experiences of the world around them. The latter refers to Vygotsky's observations about the importance of others in the process of constructing meaning, particularly the role of peers in co-constructing knowledge and the role of facilitators in creating the 'zone of proximal development', which enables the learner to build manageable units of new knowledge onto their existing knowledge base.

This is not just relevant to the early years. We all learn from direct experience and the more direct the experience, the deeper the learning. I can read about how to prune my apple tree and see it on a gardening programme on television. I can go on a course and watch an expert cut a tree in front of me. But when she challenges me to identify which branches need cutting and to pick up my pruning saw and cut them, then I have to put theory into action. With her responses to my ideas and her feedback on my practical skills, my burgeoning knowledge is facilitated. In the summer, when the fruit do or don't form and the new growth does or does not develop where I want it, then I can truly say that I have learned something about pruning apple trees. The watching and the supported action are a part of the process as is the reflection on the outcome. It takes direct experience and time to construct the learning. So it is that the earth of early years theoreticians helps construct the trunk of the social constructivist paradigm and the branch of time.

Accepting that social constructivism is the underpinning paradigm in Forest School helps to explain the gains in social and communication skills that come from participating in Forest School sessions. And constructivism expects learners to be curious and to ask questions about the real world around them. It will naturally start with the learner – their existing depth and breadth of understanding – and build from there. This style of learning gives the participants ownership of what they have found out. As they own the knowledge, they are more able to transfer it to new situations. This leads onto two more aspects of Forest School – its holistic nature and the importance of 'place', with participants returning to the same wooded site for a significant number of weeks. The holistic style of learning links to the constructivism approach – to return to my apple pruning, I am learning with my senses and my actions as well as with my mind. Classroom learning is, as Gray eloquently describes it, Cartesian in nature: 'The intelligent mind is very much separate from the functional body and that body is also separate from the world in which it exists' (Gray, 2012). Not only is this not helpful for learners, creating a learned net of isolated facts with little immediate relevance to real life, but it is also not helpful to the world of the learner, as it has little immediate relevance to his learning. The two become separate, requiring the learner to be motivated to make a further step to join them up.

The importance of a sense of place has already been mentioned in Chapter 6 and it will recur. When participants engage with a wooded space over a number of weeks, then that space becomes another key to the learning experience. The minute changes that occur from week to week as the seasons progress, as the space becomes used and as the users' perceptions sharpen, link the learner to the space as if it were another facilitator, perhaps in a more constructionist rather than constructivist model. This gives a different interpretation to the diagrammatic earth with 'Forest Education' as the place, i.e. the Forest as Education, feeding up through the social constructivist trunk, this time with the space and place as the social 'other', rather than the facilitator or peer, up to the branch of place. The pedagogy of place is significant in social geography and worthy of deeper exploration than I have space for here. The philosophical musings of Casey (2001) on the nature of the relationship between self and place emphasise the embeddedness of history and culture in place, so that my place is different to your place and it contains local elements that have relevance to me and my identity. If Forest School pedagogy embraces that link between self and place, then selecting the appropriate place for Forest School sessions becomes more than just a search for an available wood. At All Saints and at Batheaston, the children go into wild woods for their Forest School sessions. Perhaps this is one factor in their effectiveness.

The importance of time in the learning process is often mentioned by teacher trainers but in classrooms is usually ignored in favour of the importance of timetabled teaching. There is no identified 'pedagogy of time' in the academic literature. And yet, many of the case studies of Forest School activities cite time as the greatest gift the sessions bring, when children can choose to consolidate their learning through freely chosen play-based activities. It would seem that in Forest School there is a pedagogy of time, a formal recognition of its importance, not just in the insistence that sessions take place over time and that the longer the number of weeks the more lasting the effects will be. It is also recognised that activities should not be rushed; they take as long as they need to take and may be returned to in subsequent weeks. It is for the participants to decide to move on, not the leaders. If they own their learning, then only they will know when they have drained a particular activity of all it has to offer.

This chapter has begun to make explicit the pedagogy of Forest School. It is too big a topic to cover in one chapter. In the next chapter, we will consider the role of play and begin to explore the relationship between Forest School and sustainability.

GOING FORWARD

REFLECTIONS ON FOREST SCHOOL

Making explicit the pedagogy of Forest School will hopefully generate reflections and debates. In this chapter, there has been an application of Piagetian and Vygotskian theory beyond the lower primary years. There has been an acceptance of social constructivism as the underpinning paradigm in Forest School. There has been some discussion of pedagogies of place and time as critical to successful Forest School. The suggested readings below continue these themes but, like all good Forest School practice, they need to be reflected on and considered in the light of observed practice.

IDEAS FOR PRACTICE: EARTH WALKS

Some Forest School practitioners are also trained in Earth Education and have shared techniques that concentrate the senses individually on an exploration of a natural space. By focusing in on each separately, they allow participants to deepen their experience. Earth walks can be adapted for all ages and abilities. The sense exploration involves:

- sight: using a mirror to see the canopy
- touch: feel a tree and find it
- smell: identifying the scents of objects with closed eyes
- hearing: variant on sit spots
- taste: foraging.

FURTHER READING

- Clare Lamb's account of her school's integration of Forest School into a whole and holistic approach to the curriculum is inspirational: see Lamb, C. (2011) 'Forest school: a whole school approach', in Knight, S. (ed.) *Forest School for All*. London: Sage.
- Two articles which take the views of Forest School practitioners and begin to construct the pedagogy that they reveal are: O'Brien, L. (2009) 'Learning outdoors: the forest school approach', *Education 3–13*, 37(1): 45–60; and Harris, F. (2015) 'The nature of learning at forest school: practitioners' perspectives', *Education 3–13*, online only, 11 September.

- Mark Leather is both an academic and a practitioner, so his thoughts on constructionism and constructivism are a good read: Leather, M. (2012) 'Seeing the Wood from the Trees: Constructionism and Constructivism for Outdoor and Experiential Education'. Edinburgh: University of Edinburgh. Available at: http://oeandphilosophy2012.newharbour.co.uk/wp-content/uploads/2012/04/Mark-Leather.pdf
- More philosophical, and thus very thought-provoking, are the articles by Casey and Gray: Casey, E. (2001) 'Between geography and philosophy: what does it mean to be in the place-world?', *Annals of the Association of American Geographers*, 91(4): 683–93; and Gray, D.S. (2012) 'Walking in the mindfield', *International Journal of Holistic Education*, 1(1): 1–8.

9

Independent Provision Considered

This chapter considers the effects of Forest School on some schools in the independent sector in the UK, and the relationship between the pedagogy of some independent schools and Forest School. These are schools which are paid for by fees charged to the parents or by grants and bursaries from patrons and charities. The terminology of the independent sector can be rather confusing. Independent schools are privately owned and thus are in the public rather than the state sector. They may be called by any of those names: independent schools, public schools and private schools all describe the same kind of schools. Things have been further complicated by the introduction of academies which are independent of local authorities and are privately sponsored, but are in the state sector and therefore are free to attend, being paid for largely through taxation. Generally, state schools are just referred to as 'schools'. (I hope that is clear, but if not, go to www.gov.uk/types-of-school/overview.)

The benefits that accrue from attending an independent school include the fact that the class sizes are usually smaller and there is greater independence about how and what curriculum is delivered. Some disadvantages are that pupils will not learn to mix with the societal range that they will encounter in the wider world after school and indeed may be divorced from their own local communities. These factors raise questions about what education is for and how it should be achieved and are issues beyond the scope of this book.

Case Study 9.1 is of the Forest School sessions running at Gosfield School. The school appreciates the benefits of the sessions with the children in the preparatory school, which is for children aged between 5 and 11. The leader is skilled in balancing the children's freely chosen activities with introducing bushcraft skills to expand their skill repertoires and has a wonderful location in which to do this. Mature and dense woodland is interspersed with open meadowland and new tree planting – these partly as a result of the impact of Forest School, as we shall see.

CASE STUDY 9.1: A VISIT TO GOSFIELD SCHOOL FOREST SCHOOL

Gosfield School in North Essex is set in over a hundred acres of beautiful wooded parkland. It is a member of the Independent Schools Association. All pupils from early years to Year 6 have a timetabled Forest School lesson every week (www.gosfieldschool.org.uk/forest). Utilising the 110 acres of parkland, and building on the philosophy of Forest School, the school's goals are to encourage and inspire pupils through outdoor learning. From Year 7, pupils can board (live in at the school); there are also opportunities for occasional boarding and for day boarding (after-school care) to 6 pm.

I met up with Phil Davies, the school's Forest School leader, in June 2015 as he facilitated a session for a mixed group of children from classes across the preparatory school. Phil trained with the Green Light Trust in 2014 but was already experienced in teaching outdoors, with extensive bushcraft skills, as well as in teaching geography and outdoor sports. His relaxed and enabling manner has won over some initial reluctance from a few other members of staff, although the leadership team and governors were supportive and enthusiastic from the start. By the time of my visit, even more of them were already enthusiastic, whilst others were accepting that Forest School is a good idea but not for them. Phil only started running his sessions in September 2014 but such has been the success of these sessions that they will be extended over time. In his first year, the reception to Year 2 classes had whole afternoons outside, whilst Years 3–6 had only one and a half hours. This has been increased to 2–3 hours for 2015/16, an indicator of his success. The advantage of working in the private sector is that the groups are always small, something recommended for successful FS sessions. This also enables the sessions to continue for a whole year.

The successes Phil has had have convinced the school leaders that short programmes are not enough, because they have been able to see the long-term benefits already. After his first year, Phil could list some markers of success which included:

- a reception child initially unable to balance on an upturned log now climbing trees (physical and health benefits)
- a Year 5 child never having used a knife now able to split sticks with confidence (manual dexterity, hand–eye coordination, confidence)
- a Year 5 child who refused to go on the school residential camping trip has now agreed to go (emotional benefits including self-esteem and independence).

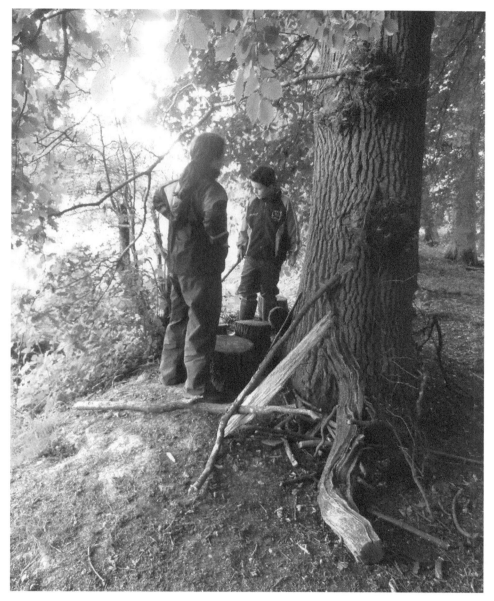

FIGURE 9.1   Role Play at Gosfield

In the group I observed, Phil had one optional leader-initiated activity – the one-spark challenge for fire lighting. The children's reflections indicated that they had taken on board that preparing for fires is key to success. The child-initiated activities I observed included 'earth boarding' (sliding down a muddy slope on a board), creating a leaf river, tree climbing, being peaceful (this involved meditating on the trees

(Continued)

(Continued)

moving in the breeze), role play as in Figure 9.1 (involving dens; this was clearly a continuation of a long-running activity that involved negotiating storylines and roles), constructing a zip wire and constructing a pulley.

Phil and I discussed whether the formal classroom curriculum 'leaked' into the Forest School. He identified two consolidations initiated by the children. One was with the Year 5s, much affected by learning about the start of the First World War, who had reconstructed some trench warfare, and included the slogan, 'It'll all be over by Christmas!' They would seem to have taken advantage of the time and space to process some complex ideas and emotions. The other was younger children rehearsing the Norman invasion and the subsequent castle-building.

At my instigation, we also talked about the children's spiritual responses to the lovely space they were occupying. Phil has a large oak tree that they have named Grandma Oak. It is situated at the entrance to a wooded area and they do ask her permission to enter. Just inside, are three younger trees nicknamed the Spice Girls (only the three who are still speaking), and these are sometimes asked instead of Grandma! When tree surgeons undertook some planned felling, the children were outraged and had to be negotiated with by surprised managers. This has led to discussion about the later mowing of some grass areas to allow seeds to set. And Phil reported that the Year 3 class had created a log circle in a dark section of the wood as a place for mystery and contemplation. It would need further investigation to unpick what of this is spiritual and what emotional (if that distinction is meaningful), but the children all indicate levels of engagement that will encourage positive attitudes towards sustainability.

Some benefits to individuals have been listed in the case study, namely those of developing personal resilience, confidence and skills. In addition, children have had time to explore their emotional reactions to the content of formal lessons and to consolidate their learning by self-initiated play-based explorations in their own time frames. They have also engaged with the school grounds at a deeper level, not just coming out for science lessons and sport but also in ways that help them to develop a sense of place. Identifying an area for mystery and contemplation also meant outrage at the proposed felling of trees. This has developed into seeking a voice so as to be more involved in planting new trees and supporting the late mowing of grassy areas to develop wild flowers and support insect life. There are four distinct benefits for the children identified by the leader: (1) using the learner-centred approach and the environment to consolidate their classroom-based learning; (2) developing a sense of place that enhances their well-being; (3) enriching their spiritual well-being by communing with the trees; and (4) increasing their awareness of sustainability issues.

This highlights another branch in the tree of Forest School pedagogy (see Figure 8.2) – that of sustainability. The children's behaviour at Gosfield, as at other schools, is a clear indicator that Forest School with its social constructivist paradigm and play-based pedagogy repeatedly occurring in the same wooded space, enables them to develop their sense of place and to care about it. This creates an engagement with sustainability at a simple and local level. It seems absurd not to recognise the importance of developing these behaviours as a part of children's normal early development, and it is one of the benefits of Forest School that this is happening. As Eernstman and Wals have found, education for sustainable development is most effective when it is embedded in 'the act of living, engaging people in place through processes' (Eernstman & Wals, 2013).

In a recent article, I reported with a colleague (Luff & Knight, 2014) on the ways in which Forest School engages children with sustainability issues using the 'Seven Rs' proposed by Pramling Samuelsson and Kaga (2010). We found that all seven were clearly embedded in Forest School pedagogy, giving children who have had that experience a grounding of engagement with these issues. The children we were discussing with practitioners were in the early primary years of their schooling, some five years before the English curriculum recognises this as an appropriate learning objective. This is not the case in Wales or Scotland, as we have seen in earlier chapters. However, in all the home countries Forest School is building the foundations of a committed engagement with sustainability issues. Without this firm foundation in the next generation, we may continue to squander our natural resources and continue with destructive practices that will ultimately end in disaster. Goulson (2014: 30) points out the importance of protecting our local wild spaces to the ultimate health of the planet, and starting local and small is exactly what Forest School sessions do.

Gosfield School is an example of how some independent schools are using Forest School sessions to complement their offering. Other independent schools offer a more alternative curriculum and two are worthy of consideration in this chapter, in that the philosophies behind them do overlap with aspects of Forest School pedagogy. Figure 8.2 continues to be useful in this context. Case Study 9.2 compares the Steiner Waldorf schools and Forest School pedagogy. The first group of schools to consider are the Steiner Waldorf schools.

CASE STUDY 9.2: STEINER PEDAGOGY CONSIDERED

Rudolf Steiner lived from 1861 to 1925, and was born in what is now Croatia, then a part of Austria. Initially, he studied both philosophy and the sciences and then worked on the writings of Goethe. Around the turn of the century, he originated the

(Continued)

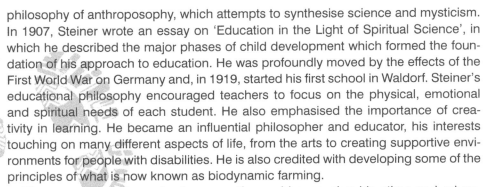

(Continued)

philosophy of anthroposophy, which attempts to synthesise science and mysticism. In 1907, Steiner wrote an essay on 'Education in the Light of Spiritual Science', in which he described the major phases of child development which formed the foundation of his approach to education. He was profoundly moved by the effects of the First World War on Germany and, in 1919, started his first school in Waldorf. Steiner's educational philosophy encouraged teachers to focus on the physical, emotional and spiritual needs of each student. He also emphasised the importance of creativity in learning. He became an influential philosopher and educator, his interests touching on many different aspects of life, from the arts to creating supportive environments for people with disabilities. He is also credited with developing some of the principles of what is now known as biodynamic farming.

There are now many schools across the world espousing his ethos and educational practices. In the UK, the 31 schools are independent, non-denominational private schools (see www.steinerwaldorf.org/). There is an emphasis on freely chosen outdoor activities that create a bond with Forest School – for example, the Cambridge Steiner School describes on its website (www.cambridge-steiner-school.co.uk/our_school/forest.html) how pupils visit the local woods at Fulbourne Fen for regular sessions, in exactly the same way as the local primary school has been doing. The emphasis on an unhurried and creative environment and a holistic approach based on the learners' interests illustrate those shared values between the two approaches, as does the use of stories and songs. However, the Steiner approach is not the same as the Forest School pedagogy offering, as it is an alternative to mainstream education, rather than a complementary addition. It is also not overtly within the social constructivist paradigm, although it can be said to embrace the importance of play, biophilia, mindfulness and time.

The Steiner approach has been influential in the ways in which many early years settings in the UK are run, valuing the individual child and their holistic needs. The influence has been less marked higher up the school age range, as we have seen in discussions of state systems. Children may move easily from a Steiner kindergarten into a state primary school but the transitions in either direction become more difficult as children grow older and they become attuned to the system they are in. There are parallels in this with the ways in which Forest School is used as children grow older, becoming less of a resource for all and more a remediation for the few. Whether the fact that it is valued at all is an indicator of something lacking in conventional teaching methods or whether it may be seen as an indicator that a child would flourish in a different education system is a point of discussion. In the UK at least, that different system is only available to those able to pay the fees the schools need, but schools are available that will follow the Steiner philosophy through to the end of school age.

Another alternative approach to education can be seen at Gordonstoun School in Elgin, Scotland. Whereas the Steiner system is available to children as young as 3 years of age, Gordonstoun takes children from the age of 8 years. The system of education espouses the outdoors, risk and challenge, and as such there are similarities with Forest School as can be seen in Case Study 9.3. However, these similarities are expressed in a more extreme way, and it is another expression of Hahn's idea, the Duke of Edinburgh's Award, which is incorporated into some Forest School sessions for older children, as we shall see in the next section.

CASE STUDY 9.3: KURT HAHN AND GORDONSTOUN SCHOOL

Kurt Hahn (1886–1974) was a key figure in the development of experiential education. In the UK, he founded the Duke of Edinburgh's Award, Gordonstoun School and Outward Bound. The motto for Gordonstoun School and the leitmotiv of his philosophy is that each of us has more courage, more strength and more compassion than we would ever have fathomed.

Hahn was raised as a Jew and in 1933 was forced to leave Germany and moved to Britain. His educational thinking was crystallised by the First World War, which he viewed as proof of the corruption of society and a promise of later doom if people could not be changed. He believed that children possess an innate decency and moral sense which is corrupted by society as they age. He believed that education could prevent this corruption, if students were given opportunities for personal leadership and to see the results of their own actions.

In 1934, he founded Gordonstoun School (www.gordonstoun.org.uk/), where the educational programme is based on four educational principles: challenge, service, internationalism and responsibility. There are some shared elements with Forest School in Hahn's ideology. They share the idea that learning is a social process, that reflection is important and that a direct relationship with the natural world refreshes the human spirit. The challenges that come from taking supported risks abut rather than overlap. Both pedagogies embrace the idea that all students need to build the confidence and capacity to take risks and meet challenges, to learn from failure, to persevere when things are hard, and to turn disabilities into opportunities. Where the differences lie are in the degree of challenge and risk typically associated with each.

To consider Figure 8.2, Hahn's ideas embrace the branches of sustainability, bushcraft, biophilia and mindfulness plus aspects of the constructivist paradigm. And although Gordonstoun offers an alternative to conventional educational practice, the Duke of Edinburgh's Award and the Outward Bound movement are complementary to it.

For parents who are uncomfortable with the state system in the UK and are unable to afford the fees of the private sector, there is the alternative of home education. This is a legal option in all parts of the UK; in England and Wales, home education is given equal status with schools under Section 7 of the Education Act 1996, which states: 'The parent of every child of compulsory school age shall cause him to receive efficient full time education suitable a) to his age ability and aptitude, and b) any special educational needs he may have, either by attendance at a school or otherwise.' And 'otherwise' refers to the right to home educate. Other parts of the UK have their own similar arrangements and since the creation of the Welsh assembly small differences have begun to develop. In particular, the pupil registration regulations in England are those passed in 2005, whilst in Wales the Welsh 2010 version is enforced. Parents who are home educating their children are often attracted by Forest School sessions, and in Chapter 14 we will mention some practitioners who are working with such children. In January 2016, *The Guardian* newspaper featured families who had taken their children out of school to learn from nature and from other cultures (Choat, 2016). Clearly, there are parents (often who are teachers by profession) who are disenchanted with the state system and are seeking alternatives, as well as schools who are looking to ameliorate the effects of that system.

In summary, the independent sector is engaging with Forest School in different ways, but without a doubt it is having an impact. Whether that is in ways similar to the state sector or on a continuum towards complete outdoor education as some parents are trying, it is a diversity of approaches that stimulates philosophical questions about the nature and purposes of education.

GOING FORWARD

REFLECTIONS ON FOREST SCHOOL

This chapter has raised philosophical questions about the purpose of education. Is it to enable the individual to be the very best that they can be? And, if so, how is that measured – by happiness, by academic achievement or by financial success? Or is it to create the citizens that a society will need to enable it to function effectively in the future? If so, how does that society decide what it will need, who will be prepared to contribute and in what way? Anyone concerned with education needs to have reflected on these questions to enable them to justify their own place in whatever system they are a part of.

IDEAS FOR PRACTICE: LEAF PRINTS (FIGURE 9.2)

This is another activity for all ages from as soon as they can wield a hammer. It works well in early autumn when the leaves have changed colour but still contain plenty of sap. Collect leaves in a range of colours and shapes. Lay thin calico or cotton, either white or unbleached, cut into squares or flag shapes over the leaves and hammer them to transfer the sap from the leaves onto the material. Use the 'prints' to make natural bunting, flags or patchwork. They will fade in sunlight, but, when they have dried initially, if you dunk them in salty water the dye lasts longer.

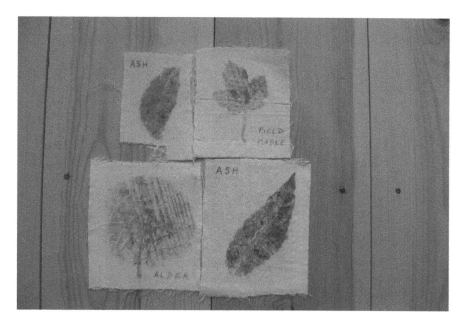

FIGURE 9.2   Leaf Prints

FURTHER READING

If you are interested in sustainability and Forest School, then read:

*   Öhman, J. & Sandell, K. (2016) 'Environmental concerns and outdoor studies', in Humberstone, B., Prince, H. & Henderson, K. (eds) *Routledge International Handbook of Outdoor Studies.* London: Routledge.

- Pramling Samuelsson, I. & Kaga, Y. (2010) 'Early childhood education to transform cultures for sustainability', in *State of the World 2010: Transforming Cultures from Consumerism to Sustainability*, 27th edn. London/New York: Worldwatch Institute.

Then try this for a light relief that carries the theme forwards:

- Goulson, D. (2014) *A Buzz in the Meadow*. London: Vintage Books.

If your interest is in the philosophy of education and Forest School, then read:

- Bailey, R., Barrow, R., Carr, D. & McCarthy, C. (eds) (2013) *The Sage Handbook of Philosophy of Education*. London: Sage.
- Quay, J. (2015) *Education, Experience and Existence: Engaging with Dewey, Peirce and Heidegger*. London: Routledge. This isn't a light read but the following quote from it should inspire you to keep going: 'More than just knowing, more than just doing, education is about being.'
- Quay, J. & Seaman, J. (2016) 'Outdoor studies and a sound philosophy of experience', in Humberstone, B., Prince, H. & Henderson, K. (eds) *Routledge International Handbook of Outdoor Studies*. London: Routledge.

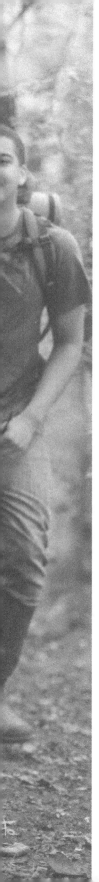

Part 4

Forest School at Secondary School

10

Forest School as Part of Special and Inclusive Education

A multisensory approach has always been a key to facilitating learning in educational provision for children with special educational needs and disabilities in the UK. People who work in specialist schools tend to be willing to explore every opportunity to help their pupils to access learning, so readers should not be surprised at how many of these schools have embraced a multisensory approach like Forest School as one of their pedagogical tools. In evaluating ways to enable children with physical disabilities to access Forest School, Hopkins (2011) encourages teachers to be more creative in their attitudes to access and inclusion, and to increase their understanding of the benefits of Forest School to children who may find a conventional approach to education unsuitable. This chapter continues that theme and explores the role of Forest School as a part of inclusive education.

In 2008, the United Nations Convention on the Rights of Persons with Disabilities (UN CRPD) came into force. It claims that it:

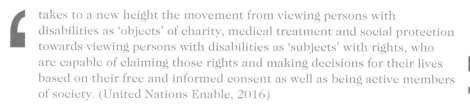

takes to a new height the movement from viewing persons with disabilities as 'objects' of charity, medical treatment and social protection towards viewing persons with disabilities as 'subjects' with rights, who are capable of claiming those rights and making decisions for their lives based on their free and informed consent as well as being active members of society. (United Nations Enable, 2016)

It was ratified by the UK Government in 2009 and informs the 2015 Special Educational Deeds and Disability Code of Practice (DfE & DoH, 2015). The new Code of Practice covers the age range of birth to 25 years, whereas its 2001 predecessor's directives ended at 19 years, and includes guidance relating to disabled children and young people as well as those with special educational needs (SEN). It echoes the UN CRPD in that it claims to have a clearer focus on the participation of children and young people and parents in decision making at individual and strategic levels. This has the potential to improve a situation where the medical, deficit, model of special needs has dominated, despite the efforts of individuals and many special schools to promote the social, person-centred model: 'Who are the most prejudiced people we encounter as parents? Not ordinary people, not other parents, but the providers of services' (cited in Rieser, 2012b). However, current budget constraints on local authorities in England are pulling services for children with particular needs in mainstream settings in the opposite direction.

What does this mean for Forest School? Forest School has been referred to as 'an enabling learning environment for children with learning difficulties, including children who have learning needs of considerable severity' (Pavey, 2006). The holistic and learner-centred nature of the approach allows for individuated experiences and meets the requirements of the UN CRPD to facilitate decision making by the participants. It is possible to enable children and young people with disabilities to enter the woods just by working with and alongside them, principally by asking them how best to provide what they need. This holds a certain amount of challenge for many teachers and Forest School leaders, who are instinctively as well as professionally protective of those they perceive as vulnerable. But, as Hopkins (2011) says, we all deserve to be able to challenge ourselves, and challenge does bring the possibility of failure. All too often, we are afraid to let vulnerable children and young people fail, and yet we know that failure can lead to personal growth. That applies to the leaders as much as to the children and young people. Returning to Figure 8.2, we can see that the social constructivist paradigm can enable the leaders to co-construct with the participants a way of accessing sessions by attending to the views of the people concerned. In addition, the freedom from time constraints that Forest School offers allows both leaders and participants to adjust their pace of doing and being to one appropriate to the interactions between the new wooded space and the learners, whoever they are and however they are abled. Being mindful of what occurs and what is observed enables leaders and participants to share and value what is achieved. Often, these achievements are about changing the perceptions of the conventionally-abled to appreciate the developing abilities of the differently-abled.

CASE STUDY 10.1: THRIFTWOOD SCHOOL

Written by Carolyn Mitchell, Cathy Nicholls and Louise Anderson

Thriftwood School (www.thriftwoodschool.com/) is a special school for children with moderate learning difficulties and complex needs. The academy consists of a school site catering for children aged 5 to 14 and a college for 15–19-year-olds. Both sites have extensive school grounds which offer many opportunities for learning outside the classroom, including a large wildlife area and allotments. Close to the school is a small wood, owned by the Chelmsford diocese, which the school manages and uses solely for Forest School. Regular opportunities are also taken to visit other local woodlands and natural spaces to benefit from the learning experiences and challenges that different environments can offer. This is possible through small class sizes and school minibuses which are part of the provision, enabling staff to maximise learning outside the classroom, offering relevant, real-life experiences.

Outdoor learning is a key feature of the whole academy, with all students taking part with a variety of staff members. Thriftwood regards itself as an 'outside school', where the outdoor environment is an important and valued aspect of the students' experience, providing space and freedom for a type of learning that is difficult to replicate indoors. Thriftwood firmly believes that all children have the right to first-hand experience of the unique and special nature of being outdoors. Students work through a progressive outdoor learning award programme that recognises their achievements from dressing appropriately for all weathers – for example, coat on, coat done up, wellies on correct feet – through to planning and carrying out a 5-mile walk. Skills, knowledge, resilience and independence are developed throughout the award programme (see Figure 10.1).

Forest School is an integral part of the outdoor learning curriculum for KS3 and a class working within a life-skills-based curriculum. There are three teachers who are Level 3 Forest School leaders and a volunteer trained as a Level 2 Forest School assistant. The school recognises the benefits of extended outdoor experiences and the ethos provided by Forest School as a powerful approach, enabling children to be:

- independent
- self-motivated
- more aware of themselves, others and the natural world
- considerate.

It sets them up for lifelong learning and particularly supports the development of:

- risk management
- problem solving
- communication

- teamwork
- self-esteem
- self-confidence.

FIGURE 10.1   January 201

(Continued)

Forest School is offered to all pupils throughout KS3, for a minimum of a term through to the whole year. Sessions run for either a whole morning or an afternoon across all seasons and embracing all weathers. Regular, consistent sessions enable pupils to practise and embed skills and knowledge and, over the three years, to make progress in a wide range of activities:

- fire building, lighting and cooking
- using tools and ropes
- playing games – team building, trust, nature awareness, competition
- physical and sensory challenges
- creating – building, craft
- singing and drama
- reflection.

Leaders are all active members of the Essex group of the Forest School Association and are committed to following Forest School principles. This is evident not only in policy, but also in practice over a number of years. This has been possible due to the conviction and support of the school leadership in investing both staff and curriculum time and money into developing, maintaining and extending Forest School with the passion and dedication of the Forest School leaders.

Over the six years that Forest School has been a part of the curriculum, the impact has been significant for holistic learning. Personal and social development is a key element for our pupils' learning, therefore our observations focus on these areas. Over time at Forest School, students demonstrate increased resilience, independence and awareness of self and others. It has also proved highly effective in the ongoing development of social communication skills, reflection and positive behaviours. Our Forest School offers a range of outdoor experiences alongside pupil-led activity sessions which are separate from the rest of the curriculum. However, our observations have shown a real link between the classroom and the outdoors, with a two-way transfer of learning and generalisation of skills. Forest School really is a powerful tool for learning at Thriftwood!

Case Study 10.1 was written by the three teachers at the school in Essex who are also trained Forest School leaders. The school has been open for over 40 years and has always had a strong outdoor learning element in its curriculum, so it might be thought that Forest School would offer nothing new to a school where there is already a range of outdoor activities from gardening to adventure opportunities. However, the staff are always looking for ways to improve their offering and, for six years now, Forest School has been a part of the school's outdoor learning curriculum, and the three teachers who were already skilled as teachers of children with additional needs have added training as Forest School leaders to their portfolios. In addition, one of the learning assistants has also undertaken Level 2 training, which is at assistant level.

Forest School is delivered principally to the children in Key Stage 3. This means that the children's chronological age is roughly from 11 to 14 years old. As they point out, the leaders have focused on recording the outcomes for personal and social development, but also note the transferrable skills that relate to classroom learning. Six years is long enough to be able to claim that Forest School is highly effective for the children and young people at the school, and that it has earned its place in the outdoor curriculum.

As can be seen in the case study, the activities that the children choose from are the same as those already mentioned for other ages and groups. The sessions are similarly set up, with time to progressively transfer the ownership and leadership from the leaders to the young people as the weeks pass, and with the leaders offering instruction in specific skills to support the children's goals. This immersive experience in wooded spaces develops exactly the same skills for these learners as for the groups previously discussed – namely, social communication skills, increased resilience, independence and awareness of self and others. Even in a school already using nature and the outdoors in a wide range of activities, the experience of Forest School offers something different and valuable. The combination of trees (place), time, bushcraft and mindfulness held in the paradigm of social constructivism speaks to our biophilia and helps sustain these learners, as illustrated in Figure 8.2.

The area of social communication is of primary importance when working with learners on the autistic spectrum. All Forest School leaders bring their own particular skills and previous learning to their Forest School sessions, and in the case of Burrows (2011) it is his training as an art and eco-therapist that he brings to his work and to his research. He has found that young adults on the autistic spectrum can find transferrable ways of working and communicating together through art-based activities at Forest School (ibid. 2012). When observing one of his sessions, it is clear that place is important – the trees offer a diffused light that is more manageable than brighter lighting to many on the spectrum, and a seclusion and quiet that minimise the sensory overload they may experience in a conventional learning space. Time is also a key element as each learner can take their own time to consider every move and interaction. Burrows provided materials to stimulate artistic activities, often to do with mask making, but I observed that his own interactions with the learners were slow, minimal and based on careful observation. His work is a demonstration of the value of incorporating different specialisms, where appropriate, into Forest School work, whilst maintaining the key ethos. Recognising when and where working in partnership with other experts, or where personal development, is needed, is important for Forest School leaders working with vulnerable others.

The Forest School Association (FSA) is allied to the Index for Inclusion Network which promotes a commitment to particular values aiming to overcome exclusion and promote participation. It states that:

"values are fundamental guides and prompts to action … For all actions affecting others are underpinned by values" (www.indexforinclusion.org/avaluesframework.php). The values of Forest School should ensure that all learners are welcomed into the woods:

At Forest School all participants are viewed as:

- equal, unique and valuable
- competent to explore and discover
- entitled to experience appropriate risk and challenge
- entitled to choose, and to initiate and drive their own learning and development
- entitled to experience regular success
- entitled to develop positive relationships with themselves and other people
- entitled to develop a strong, positive relationship with their natural world.

This learner-centred approach interweaves with the ever-changing moods and marvels, potential and challenges of the natural world through the seasons to fill every Forest School session and programme with discovery and difference. Yet, each programme does also share a common set of principles, aimed at ensuring that all learners experience the cumulative and lasting benefits that quality Forest School offers. (FSA, 2016b)

In Figure 0.2 in the Introduction, the survey of practitioners shows that of those questioned 5 per cent are working with children and young people with special educational needs or disabilities and a further 3 per cent are working with children and young people with behavioural difficulties. Whilst these are not high percentages compared with the 49 per cent who are working with children of preschool age, it is important to note that such groups are serving a much smaller population. In the 2015 National Statistics, only 2.8 per cent of children were recorded as having a statement of special educational needs or an Education, Health and Care Plan (DfE, 2015), equating to 236,165 pupils. Whilst it is unlikely that all children and young people with special educational needs or disabilities have access to Forest School sessions, the probability is higher for them than it is for other children of similar ages. As we will see in the next chapter, the majority of children of secondary school age will only encounter Forest School sessions if they fall into a group identified as being in need of extra support.

REFLECTIONS ON FOREST SCHOOL

Forest School leaders are trained to foster a learner-led environment that will enhance children's decision-making opportunities. When working with children and young people with special educational needs or disabilities, some may find this a greater challenge than others. Hart's Ladder of Participation has been influential in supporting training in this area and has been subsequently reworked by Shier (2001) to provide 15 questions for practitioners to evaluate their planning for participation. These start with 'Are you ready to listen to children?' and end with 'Is it a policy requirement that children and adults share power and responsibility for decisions?' Somewhere in the middle is the minimum point which play workers need to be working at to meet the requirements of the UN Convention on the Rights of the Child (Committee on the Rights of the Child, 1995). When working with children and young people with special educational needs or disabilities, there can be a need for creative ways to facilitate children's participation. Make a list of all the conditions that children and young people with special educational needs or disabilities may have, and mark those that may require imagination in order to facilitate participation. Brainstorm ways that you could use to make it happen.

IDEAS FOR PRACTICE: LEAF ART (FIGURES 10.2–10.4)

Autumn leaves are a wonderful stimulus to creativity. At the 2015 FSA conference, the delegates gathered leaves and created an array of responses. There is room for just three here to stimulate your imagination.

FIGURE 10.2   Labyrinth

FIGURE 10.3   Colours

FIGURE 10.4   Nest

FURTHER READING

- We are fortunate now in having people with particular needs and disabilities who are prepared to articulate what it feels like to struggle with the systems that are supposed to support their education. Read:
  - Rieser, R. (2012a) 'Inclusive education', in Cole, M. (ed.) *Education, Equality and Human Rights*. London: Routledge.
  - Rieser, R. (2012b) 'The Struggle for Inclusion: The Growth of a Movement'. Available at http://worldofinclusion.com/articles/
- To learn more about the Forest School work already being done with children and young people with special educational needs or disabilities, read:
  - Hopkins, F. (2011) 'Removing barriers: getting children with physical challenges into the woods', in Knight, S. (ed.) *Forest School for All*. London: Sage.
  - Pavey, B. (2006) 'The Forest School and Inclusion: A Project Evaluation'. Available at www.leeds.ac.uk/educol/documents/161165.htm
- To consider how to increase children's participation in decision making, read:
  - Shier, H. (2001) 'Pathways to participation: openings, opportunities and obligations', *Children & Society*, 15: 107–17.

11

Forest School as an Intervention Strategy in Mainstream Schools

Perhaps it is the way in which Forest School has developed from an initial early years focus at Bridgwater College to an intervention strategy for pupils with behavioural issues or learning difficulties. Or perhaps it is the nature of the secondary school curriculum, segmented into separate subjects, focused on exam success and with little space for natural holistic human development. For whatever reason, Forest School sessions for children attending secondary school tend to have a specific focus and a definite purpose. In this chapter, we will consider what these focuses may be, what the outcomes of Forest School sessions are perceived to be and how they are implemented. As our case study, we will use the Plas Derw Trust in North Wales. Like so many independent providers, the Trust offers a range of sessions to clients, from working with early years groups to develop their own Forest School sessions and training practitioners, to running sessions for all age groups. This model can be found across the UK where trained and experienced practitioners work with communities both to provide Forest School sessions and to expand provision through training and development. In the case study, we cite three ways in which Plas Derw work with children of secondary school age.

CASE STUDY 11.1: PLAS DERW TRUST

Plas Derw Trust (www.plasderwforestschool.co.uk) is located on the Northop Campus of Glyndwr University in Flintshire, North Wales (see Figure 11.1).

The Trust's Forest School activities are many and various, ranging from a toddler group to 'Tranquil Tuesdays' for adults with mental health issues, from training courses for practitioners to holiday clubs for children of all ages. Of interest to this chapter are the three projects run for children of secondary school age.

The first of these is a project to support children making the transition between primary and secondary school. The sessions allow children to form relationships with peers in a relaxed environment and to feel more secure and confident in their new setting.

The second project is to promote inclusion at a local high school. Initially grant funded by various bodies, five young adults who are on the autistic spectrum join five youngsters of a similar age from another mainstream school. They work together in the woods, and it has given the children from the high school a greater understanding and appreciation of diversity than they had before. For both groups, it has raised their self-esteem and given them a sense of achievement. The schools have recognised the value of the project to the extent that, when the funding was cut, they continued to support it and have found the funds to keep it going.

The third and final project is for children leaving school at the end of Year 11 with few GCSEs, and is designed to give them confidence and a sense of purpose for their next phase of education or training.

FIGURE 11.1   The View from the Trust

The first example involves a group of sessions designed to smooth the transition from one educational setting to another. We have already mentioned briefly a transition group on the Isle of Wight (Case Study 8.2) and made reference in Chapter 6 to the description by Horning (2011) of a similar group in Scotland. In all three cases, the children have been identified by their primary schools as being likely to find the move from primary to secondary school a challenge. In the UK, primary schools can be very small depending on their location, particularly in rural areas, whereas secondary schools have grown in size so that typically they will cater for an intake that is at least three times as many children in each year as there are in their feeder primaries, and the children will certainly be aged 11–16, sometimes to 18, so the difference in the physical size of the children can be huge, as well as the difference in the number of bodies moving around the school. As a result, some children can find the move daunting, resulting either in difficulties in learning or in making the social connections they will need. This can lead to unwanted behaviours or in children failing to make educational or social progress.

Children with this difficulty in transitioning may have an extremely rural background so that their experience of socialising in large groups is potentially limited. It may be that they are perceived to have an academic profile outside the normal range, above or below, so that peers might not accept them readily into their social groups. Or there may be other factors that mark them out as 'different'. As a species, we have a sensitivity to difference that leads us to stereotyping and, through that, to rejection. When we were a physically weak species surviving on the savannahs of Africa, this was a useful survival strategy, enabling us to identify quickly whether fight, flight or friendship was the best way forward. Now that we live in large and very mixed communities, it is a potentially destructive instinct and we do not need to be the servants of our instincts. Unfortunately, 'ontogenesis echoes phylogenesis', and 11-year-old children encountering a new territory where they need to establish their positions in new classroom hierarchies are liable to revert to their primal instincts. As adults, we can work with the majority to school them into managing both their transition and their instincts, but the minorities also need our extra help and that is where Forest School comes in.

The purposes of these sessions include enabling children to make some friendships that will support them in the initial period of transition and helping them to develop sufficient resilience to give them the inner strength they may need. Typically, these pupils will be in a group drawn from more than one primary school, so the Forest School leader will be scaffolding the formation of new social contacts, skills that will be transferable, and building the self-confidence and self-esteem that create resilience and which have already been established as measurable outcomes of Forest School. The first few sessions will usually be about exploring the wooded space and creating a base camp, getting to know each other and establishing boundaries, particularly which areas can be freely explored and which require the participants to negotiate how far they can go on their own and how long they can stay away from the group leaders. Another primitive instinct is useful here. Children are pre-programmed not to go too far from their supervising adults in the same way that the vulnerable young of any species will stay close to their guarding elders for reasons of survival. And what is important in the early sessions is the building of a strong trust between all the participants, both the children and the facilitator, and the establishing of a sense of place encircled and nurtured by trees.

Once the participants are all settled in their space, with a sense of community and place, the facilitator can help the children to explore further. This is a delicate relinquishing of leadership to achieve a more democratic balance. The leader may bring tools and ideas to sessions, and the children will bring their interests and their curiosity. The leader will support the learning of new skills like fire lighting, tree climbing and whittling, and the children will share discoveries and adventures. Exactly what the activities are will vary according to the children's interests and the practitioner's skills. What the activities are is not as important as offering the children interesting and appropriate achievable challenges that help them to grow their confidence and self-esteem. Alongside this are the 'ways of being' that deepen their resilience. Developing mindfulness may be achieved both by introducing 'sit spot' time for meditation in and on nature and by reflective sessions around the campfire. The community grows stronger, more confident, more communicative. As Beames and Brown (2016) identify, adventurous learning equips young people to deal with a constantly changing world, and those adventures come in many shapes and sizes. Uncertainty, agency, authenticity and mastery are the elements that Beames and Brown cite as being key to adventurous learning, and they can all be present in these Forest School sessions. Increasingly, the children lead on what will happen in sessions and are confident to engage in their own activities separately when they wish to. Visiting an established group like this is a joy, as it will brim with curiosity and warmth.

The groups that form for such a defined purpose will, of necessity, be limited to a specific number of sessions, hopefully at least 10. Regrettably, it is the schools rather than the leaders who decide on the number of sessions they are prepared to fund, so leaders need to be articulate in communicating the importance of repeating sessions. The greater the number of sessions, the stronger the changes will be and the more likely they are to be permanent, as neural pathways are established and mylanised, as described in Chapter 1. However many there are, the last two will have to be used in part to prepare the children for their ending. What has been co-created can have a deep impact and it would be destructive on many levels to end the sessions abruptly. It is therefore important for the leader to undertake preparatory features, such as introducing into the reflections a focus on what skills the children think they will take away with them when they move on. This will help prepare them, as will meditating on natural images in the woods to store them in the memory.

The second type of sessions mentioned in the case study are those offered to a mixture of students with special learning needs and students within the average range of abilities. The purposes here are to increase the confidence and self-esteem of the former group and the tolerance and understanding of the latter. In the UK, societal goals have for many years been about integrating people across the full ability range into mainstream society, but all too often as adults they are excluded not by an ability deficit, as is indicated by the case study in Chapter 10, but by the attitudes of those living around them. Rieser (2012a: 193) includes ignoring, bullying and devaluing in these as well as lack of empowerment. This project aims to spread understanding and tolerance through working together for mutual empowerment.

The process of forming the group and following their interests is very similar to that described above, with a couple of differences. One is that the group forms for a whole academic year, to give longer for changes to be secure in both groups. The other is that the initial integration period may be a week or so longer, to allow the two groups of students to get used to each other. The outcomes have been as desired, and the project has become embedded as an ongoing one. Over time, indeed years, the effects should be felt across the wider local community as the two groups of students reach adulthood and greater independence. Forest School is not about quick fixes but about deep change and education for sustainability, both human and natural.

The third example in the case study is of Forest School sessions with older pupils who are likely to leave school with few GCSEs and a restricted set of goals. The sessions aim to raise their aspirations by increasing their confidence and self-esteem, and develop their skills, both practical and communicative. The state education system is notoriously unhelpful to those whose skills are not conventionally academic. Gardner (cited in Lucas et al., 2013: 34) identified many forms of intelligence, but the UK system favours only those students able to pass written theoretical tests. As a result, those students who are differently gifted can leave school with low self-worth and few ideas for the future. As has been shown, Forest School is ideally suited to raising confidence and self-esteem and can include activities suited to a range of abilities and interests.

Bushcraft is a key branch in the Forest School pedagogical tree (see Figure 8.2) and all Forest School practitioners are required to have a minimum level of competency in key bushcraft skills such as tying knots and sharpening tools. However, basic training does only cover this basic level, so it is incumbent upon practitioners to undertake such further training as is relevant to the groups they may be working with. As the client groups include older students who may wish to engage in a wider range of activities, so the bushcraft skills of the leaders become more important. The balancing of the different aspects of Forest School pedagogy is a continual responsibility of the Forest School leader, who needs to be sensitive to the emotional needs of the group and the best ways to meet these, in working with the full panoply of options in their natural wooded space. Bushcraft skills are tools towards an end rather than an end in themselves, but for students in this group they may also offer an insight into future opportunities.

Modern apprenticeships in the UK in heritage and conservation skills are becoming available through such bodies as the Heritage Craft Alliance and the Forestry Commission. Some Forest School practitioners, including Plas Derw, are offering certification for skills such as 'Forest School Level 1 Award', 'Practical Conservation Skills' and 'Sustainable Woodland Management'. These may enable students to seek apprenticeships that may lead to work opportunities. Whilst this is not the primary role of Forest School leaders, it may be a valid, indeed important, option for some members of groups such as these. For others, the opportunity for reflection in a wooded space supported by sympathetic leaders and the soothing effects of trees, tuning in to that which Deakin calls 'the natural kinship between human beings and woods' (2008: 44), may help them to see a more positive future for themselves after their school career ends.

As we have shown, Forest School has much to offer children in the secondary school age group. It is a shame for the majority of these children that access is restricted to such a small section of that community. Beames and Brown (2016) challenge secondary school teachers in both the outdoor and indoor sector to examine their practice for true adventurousness. I hope we have shown that the spirit of Forest School pedagogy is to allow for their stated four key elements of uncertainty, agency, authenticity and mastery.

GOING FORWARD

REFLECTIONS ON FOREST SCHOOL

Having stated that good Forest School practice is, by its nature, about adventurous learning, I now challenge Forest School leaders to reflect on their own practice and make sure that their delivery is just that. Do you promote the four key elements of uncertainty, agency, authenticity and mastery? How would you prove that to a visitor to your sessions? Use Figure 8.2 to interrogate your practice and inform your answers. If you are not yet a Forest School leader, then arrange a visit to a session, and, if you cannot see uncertainty, agency, authenticity and mastery happening, then ask the leader to explain it to you.

IDEAS FOR PRACTICE: DEN MAKING (FIGURE 11.2)

This activity can have many purposes from role play to overnight survival, and so can be approached in a variety of ways. It is a fundamental urge of most participants to create a base with a shelter of some kind. The very basic shelter illustrated was erected by 4-year-olds with minimal supervision and uses a tarpaulin. A group of 6-year-old girls I worked with made 30 cm-high shelters for their Barbie dolls with sticks and grasses. Teenagers, and, indeed, trainee Forest School leaders, can make bivouacs from natural materials that will provide warmth and shelter. Wicks (2011: 159) demonstrates an evolution in den making that is about emotional development more than skill development. I visited Umeå University in Sweden and observed trainee teachers making snow holes to spend the night in. Experimentation and creativity should be encouraged when the risk of exposure is low!

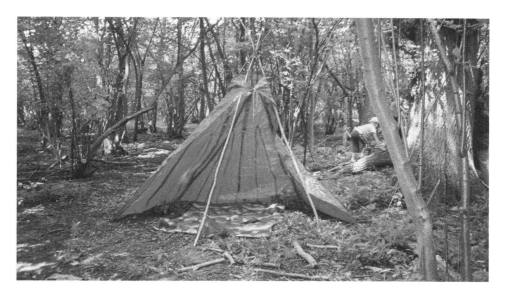

FIGURE 11.2   My Den

FURTHER READING

- Try two readings about different particular needs: Wicks, R. (2011) 'Forest school and looked after children', in Knight, S. (ed.) *Forest School for All*. London: Sage, is mentioned above in respect of den making; and Rieser, R. (2012a) 'Inclusive education', in Cole, M. (ed.) *Education, Equality and Human Rights*. London: Routledge, discusses the failings in the UK education system.

- A whole new book about the pedagogy of adventure, and exploring what adventure means in respect of learning, is Beames, S. & Brown, M. (2016) *Adventurous Learning: A Pedagogy for a Changing World*. London: Routledge.
- Compare two chapters from the same book: Prince, H. & Exeter, D. (2016) 'Formal curricular initiatives and evaluation in the UK', in Humberstone, B., Prince, H. & Henderson, K. (eds) *Routledge International Handbook of Outdoor Studies*. London: Routledge, discusses outdoor education in the UK; whilst Ho, S., Atencio, M., Tan, Y. & Ching, C. (2016) 'The inclusion of outdoor education in the formal school curriculum', in Humberstone et al., considers new developments in outdoor education in Singapore. It is possible to read for signs of uncertainty, agency, authenticity and mastery in each system and to use one to deepen your understanding of the other.
- Just enjoy reading Deakin, R. (2008) *Wildwood: A Journey through Trees*. London: Penguin, and absorb the author's reflections on the importance of trees to human life.

12

Forest School and Pupil Referral Units

This chapter will consider how Forest School can help young people who have been failed by the mainstream education system. One member of the original Bridgwater group who started Forest School in the UK then left the college and started up his own centre where many of his groups were children and young people, mostly boys, with behavioural difficulties. Gordon Woodall rewrote the original Forest School training course, validated through BTEC, with its early years focus to include learning outcomes relating to emotional intelligence in the new course validated by the Open College Network. His interest in the work of Goleman (1996) and how to help children and young people relearn self-control, motivation and persistence has led to Forest School being offered as a suitable intervention for children and young people who struggle in mainstream settings. Some of these learners will already have been transferred from those mainstream schools to pupil referral units (PRU) and may have complex and challenging emotional and behavioural difficulties.

Both Goleman (1996) and Sunderland (2013) point to impaired brain development as a result of relational poverty or stress, particularly in early childhood. Sunderland claims that this leads to underdeveloped frontal lobes, which is where our abilities to control and reflect on our feelings lie, as well as our abilities to concentrate and learn. In addition, these children and young people can have over-sensitive stress response systems, causing them to be irritable, anxious and angry. The exclusions they experience from schools that are at a loss as to how to manage their behaviours only increase their feelings of alienation and anger. As Dorling (2016) says, 'Being ostracised is one of the most severe punishments humans inflict on each other.'

What Forest School practitioners working with such children are trying to do is two-fold. First, there are beneficial effects from being in any green space on the emotional well-being of each person. These are being recorded in a range of studies (for example, Aspinall et al., 2013; Roe et al., 2013). Second, there are the long-term changes in behaviour that are being recorded specifically from Forest School sessions that indicate changes in the brain of each of the participants. This requires attendance at enough sessions to effect that change, which may be measured in years rather than weeks.

Archard (2015) has recorded findings from a project being carried out in Somerset, published on the Good from Woods website (www.goodfromwoods. co.uk). This site is the outcome of Good from Woods, which was a National Lottery-funded research project led by the Silvanus Trust and Plymouth University, in partnership with the Woodland Trust, Neroche Scheme and Forest Research. It started in April 2010 and ran until December 2014 to develop a toolkit to promote practitioner research. It offers practitioners guidance on how to set up and record research projects. As can be seen from Archard (2015), it is effective and will offer academics data to work on when collating the benefits of interventions such as Forest School.

Some of the children in Archard's study have been attending sessions for four years, some for only six weeks, demonstrating the project's responsiveness to individual needs. Her key findings are three-fold. First, she identifies the importance of play at all ages. Hughes (2012) combines concepts from cognitive psychology and evolutionary biology to develop the idea of evolutionary playwork, which he claims suggests a relationship between the drive to play and the development of the mind. This would not seem unlikely; as an adaptive species with the capacity to create unique solutions to problems, we need an environment that prompts us to the kind of 'fiddling about' (play) that leads to discoveries and understandings. As a social species, we do this best in groups. So in Archard's groups play is the vehicle for social interactions and allows the participants to learn to negotiate and form relationships in non-threatening conditions. They also have some control over their sessions – something that may not occur outside Forest School. That sense of control and those social relationships provide opportunities for growth and change.

Archard's second key finding is the importance of Forest School as a space where different rules apply. She implies that in this different space the young people and the adults who work with them were able to rework their relationships without the constraints placed on them by a more formal school setting. More physicality was involved than is usual in school settings, and this may link to a need to communicate non-verbally if past verbal communications have been problematic, and to create healthier attachments with the staff who are involved in their everyday schooling. Building a new bond of trust can create a new platform for work outside the Forest School sessions, even where the formality has to be returned to. There are echoes here of the work of the Nurture Group Network (https://nurturegroups.org/about-us), where the aim is to create developing warm and accepting relationships with teachers and peers. This encourages the rebuilding of those emotional skills that have been affected by damaging early experiences and positive ways to communicate and interact with others. Some nurture groups do indeed use Forest School sessions to support this process. These initiatives underline the key role of attachment in healthy human development. Early research by Bowlby and Ainsworth emphasised the importance of attachment for healthy development in young children, but later research by Hazan and Shaver has considered the impact on adults as well, on a continuum from those who form ambivalent adult relationships through to those displaying 'reactive attachment disorder', a disorder that requires psychological interventions. In Archard's sessions, the young adults and those working with them are reworking their attachments to create healthier relationships now and hopefully giving the young people the tools to form these with others in the future.

The last finding relates to what is described as a 'natural connection', enabling the young people to build a relationship with the natural environment. There are several strands to this finding. Archard mentions the importance of acquiring the language to do this. If we have the words to understand and share what we are seeing and doing, it is easier for us to store the memories we are building. Then there is the biophilia hypothesis (Kellert & Wilson, 1993) – that as humans we need a healthy bond with nature for the sake of our own health, physical and mental. And there are our sustainability needs, both social and environmental. When young people feel a connection with nature and each other, they will care for both.

Jon Cree, the chairman of the Forest School Association (FSA), wrote a description of the Bishops Wood Centre's work with 14–19-year-old boys in 2011 (Cree, 2011). The Bishops Wood Centre, whilst still owned by Worcestershire County Council, is now run by the Field Studies Council. Its range of courses and services is still extensive (see www.worcestershire.gov.uk/info/20018/bishops_wood_centre), but many are now full-cost recovery. Five years later, the centre is still carrying out the important work Jon is involved in, even though the framework around it has changed. In Case Study 12.1, Jon updates his thoughts on the work of the centre.

CASE STUDY 12.1: 'ALTERNATIVE' FOREST SCHOOL AND OUTDOOR/VOCATIONAL EDUCATION PROVISION – THE CHALLENGES FIVE YEARS ON

Written by Jon Cree

'Environments in which child and therapist interact and participate, plus the relationship they develop and the embodied meanings they enact together provide the path that leads to the pathway of change' (Santostefano, 2004: 164).

In the chapter I contributed to Sara Knight's book in 2011, I outlined some of the ways we work with adolescents whose needs are not met by mainstream schools, and try to combine this with vocational qualifications – using a Forest School learner-centred approach. Since then, Bishops Wood Centre, run by Worcestershire County Council, has continued with our so-called 'alternative provision' and it has grown. This label says it all to me in terms of how this type of learning is viewed in our education system, i.e. 'this is not generally acceptable' and it is seen as some sort of compensatory education. Two educational system structural changes have happened in England since 2011, and, in my opinion, have contributed further to this decline in stature for this type of 'embodied' vocational learning. They are:

- the slimming down of vocational subjects acknowledged as GCSE equivalents by a large percentage, after the Wolf Report was published in 2011. This meant that the majority of vocational qualifications no longer counted towards a school's league table score. The effect of this was a decline in the provision of vocational education for the 14–16 age group
- the raising of the school age, from 16 to 18, in which students should be in full-time education or training, introduced in 2014.

My impressions are that schools are referring pupils even more because there is a lack of resources and 'alternative' provision in the school – because it is no longer recognised. There is an increasing number of a minority of students whose needs are not being met. This is resulting in more students with emotional and behavioural needs not being catered for. At Bishops Wood, for example, we are experiencing more individual referrals for Looked after Children and young people with specific needs from secondary schools. The outdoor provision is seen as either a place to re-engage learners – as cited by Santostefano in his groundbreaking book in 2004 – or a place to get the students out of the restricting school environment in which they can be seen as disruptive.

There is a growing body of evidence that shows that regular exposure to the natural world can provide a 'pathway of change' towards increased engagement in learning, healthy brain development, increased self-awareness/self-worth and healthy relational development (Selhub & Logan, 2014). This is a positive move if the provision is integrated and valued by the education institution and teachers. By valued, I mean that they embrace the approach taken by a Forest School practitioner, which follows what Alfie Kohn frames as the 3 Cs – working with Choice, creating an equal learning Community, and providing learning that has appropriate, meaningful Content and Context (Kohn, 2006). With this growing need, it does beggar the question, what happened to 'Every Child Matters'? It seems to me they only matter if they are gaining A–Cs in their GCSEs, or the EBacc, and it makes this integration into the school of 'alternative provision' even harder than just five years ago.

It has not been helped by the loss of all the land-based qualifications and units from the vocational qualifications that contribute to school performance tables. And these qualifications do require a certain level and type of literacy that many of the learners we are working with do not have. While we do need that basic literacy to survive in this modern world, the way this is measured can be limiting. Many of our learners are often very articulate, however when it comes to paperwork then the paper phobia, associations and often learning difficulties associated with the A4 sheet can be a huge barrier. This leaves only the 'preparation for life and work' awards from smaller awarding bodies. The flexibility and range of units offered that are in the national framework and are therefore approved by the Office of Qualifications and Examinations Regulation (Ofqual) mean that they can work with the students' interests. They cover generic skills such as communication, teamwork and personal development, plus horticulture, woodland management, woodworking, creating craft objects from natural materials, and others. Also, there are a number of 'awards' that are available and can be tailored to both Forest School's conservation aims and the learners' development, such as the John Muir Award, ASDAN, Duke of Edinburgh, and some local authorities and organisations have their own awards – all of which can contribute to a student portfolio.

Another challenge has been the ever-growing complexity of the psychological needs of teenagers. There has been much 'noise' made by the mental health profession and indeed the government (see the Mental Health Taskforce report published by Mind, 2016). Indeed, the statistics and stories on teenagers with mental health issues and how these grow into adulthood are alarming – see www.huffingtonpost.co.uk/2016/02/11/we-spoke-to-adults-with-mental-health-issues_n_9207882.html. In the 'Children of the New Century' report, published by the Centre for Mental Health and UCL Institute of Education in November 2015, the statistics for teenage mental health raise huge concerns – an estimated 28 per cent of 11-year-olds' parents stated that their child had severe difficulties with at least one of four major mental health behaviours – conduct problems, hyperactivity/inattention, emotional problems and peer problems. So, what does this mean for Forest School/outdoor 'alternative' education provision? Two key factors come to my mind – one is that often practitioners are not trained/equipped to deal with the increasing complexity of issues – after all, many FS practitioners are not trained eco-/psycho- or play therapists. Sometimes, I have witnessed provision sailing close to the 'wind' with both emotional and physical safety. The other is that we often do not have the capacity to follow through with other agencies, or indeed with teachers in schools, on the invaluable work carried

(Continued)

(Continued)

out and 'embodied' in the woods. After all, this is where the learner-centred, needs-based approach often results in embodied behaviour that is both appropriate and progressive, as expressed in my chapter in 2011. So, I leave you with two related questions that are currently in my mind: (1) Where do we draw the line with the type of learners presented to us at Forest School; and (2) If a line has to be drawn, what support do we need to work effectively with the increasing needs that our learners are presenting so that line can be extended?

Work with students aged 14–19 is mostly with boys who are struggling with the education system and who have been excluded or are non-attenders. Jon's team uses the structure of Forest School sessions as already described to frame work around developing the students' emotional intelligence and sometimes enabling them to achieve a vocational award in practical woodland and land-based skills. Doing this requires that tutors have the requisite skills and teaching abilities themselves. In addition, they require the patience, vigilance and nurturing skills of Forest School leaders, but in very large amounts! The work is slow: achieving a Level 1 certificate takes one to two years and students may not be ready to sign up to undertake such a programme when they first come to the centre.

Jon identifies the students' need for a positive role model who can help them to create and recreate the synaptic links and neural pathways that may not have been formed appropriately in their earlier years of development (Cree, 2011). Doing this requires trust and time – something that is constantly under threat from budget cuts and political manoeuvering. To help schools and units to evidence the progress that will protect their funding, the centre provides weekly and termly reports as well as working towards recognised National Open College Network (NOCN) awards with young people who may not achieve any other qualifications.

From consulting with and reading about Forest School practitioners working with these young people, and from considering the work of psychologists such as Margot Sunderland, it is clear that the roots of the behavioural difficulties the young people are experiencing lie in their formative early years. To help offer a secure start, parents in Scotland in 2016 began a campaign (www.upstart.scot/) to raise the school starting age to 7, in line with the most successful Western nations' education systems in Finland, Estonia and Switzerland. Sue Palmer published a book on the same theme in 2016 (Palmer, 2016). By the time the young people come to Jon, Jenny Archard and others, they have had years of deteriorating relationships and school performance, and the damage will take years to repair. If the problems were sorted out at an earlier stage, we could be dealing with a whole person not a repaired one.

GOING FORWARD

REFLECTIONS ON FOREST SCHOOL

Consider Jon's questions: 'Where do we draw the line with the type of learners presented to us at Forest School; and if a line has to be drawn, what support do we need to work effectively with the increasing needs that our learners are presenting so that line can be extended?' Consider what support you would need to enable you to help these young people.

IDEAS FOR PRACTICE: WILLOW WEAVING

Working with older children and young adults often requires suggesting activities that can be accessed at a wide range of starting abilities. Willow weaving is just such an activity and needs only a pair of secateurs to accomplish. At a simple level, a long piece of willow can be twisted into a circle which can be decorated as a crown, a camouflage helmet or a hanging decoration for a door. Another simple activity is to make a hurdle to shelter from the wind in the sitting area (see Figure 12.1).

FIGURE 12.1   A Willow Hurdle

Other willow weaving requires that the harvested stems be kept damp to preserve their flexibility. This is less important for a hurdle, and, indeed, they can be made with a range of materials. Stick sharpened uprights into the ground at about 30 cm intervals. If you offset them, you create a space to fill with brush (and the sticks may need to be closer together); if the line is straight, you will be able to weave the willow and create something more long-lasting.

FIGURE 12.2   A Willow Green Man

At the other end of the willow-weaving scale are works of art such as the Green Man in Figure 12.2. This obviously needs planning and design, but it shows the range of activities that can be encompassed. The hare in Figure 12.3 took a long morning to create and needs the legs to be fixed in place in a box or in the ground until it has dried out, which can take weeks not days.

There is a range of books with ideas for willow weaving that include baskets and the ubiquitous domes so popular with schools. If the time of year is right (spring) and the earth damp enough, willow will strike just by sticking a stem in the ground. It also grows at a prodigious speed which is why so many school domes and tunnels have become unruly and unused. Trimming these and weaving in the long growths to cover the gaps or to build extensions is another absorbing task best done in groups.

FIGURE 12.3   A Willow Hare

FURTHER READING

- Read more about the two groups discussed in this chapter:

  - Archard, J. (2015) 'The Impact of Regular Forest School Sessions on Young Teenagers' Wellbeing'. Torpoint: Silvanus Trust. Available at https://goodfrom woods.wordpress.com/case-studies/
  - Cree, J. (2011) 'Maintaining the forest school ethos while working with 14–19-year-old boys', in Knight, S. (ed.) *Forest School for All*. London: Sage.

- The notes from Sunderland's talk to the FSA conference are almost identical to those given to the UNICEF conference and are accessible to all: Sunderland, M. (2012) 'The Science of Parenting', notes from lecture given at the Baby Friendly Initiative Conference 2012 and available at http://unicef.org.uk/Documents/ Baby_Friendly/Conference/Presentations/2012/Parenting_Margot_Sunderland_ BFI_Conf_2012.pdf
- Studies on the effects of attachment to fathers as well as mothers are less common. Grossman and Grossmann carried out their first research in the 1980s, and

here it is updated: Grossmann, K. & Grossmann, K. (2007) 'The impact of attachment to mother and father at an early age on children's psychosocial development through young adulthood', in *Encyclopedia on Early Childhood Development*. Montreal: Centre of Excellence for Early Childhood Development. Available at www.child-encyclopedia.com/Pages/PDF/GrossmannANGxp_rev.pdf

- Sue's new book echoes the concerns of many in the UK about the effects of being too formal too early: Palmer, S. (2016) *Upstart: The Case for Raising the School Starting Age and Providing what the Under-Sevens Really Need*. Edinburgh: Floris Books.

Part 5

Other Forest School Occurrences

13

Improving Mental Health

Given the recorded successes in improving children's mental health with Forest School sessions (for example, Acton & Carter, 2016; Box, 2015; Roe et al., 2008), it is not surprising that some practitioners are now offering Forest School to adults with mental health issues. As there has been more research done on the effects of nature on adults than on children, this offers opportunities as well as challenges to the Forest School community – opportunities to use existing research to interrogate and analyse Forest School practice and challenges in the magnitude of the tasks some practitioners are proposing to accept and the ethical dimensions involved.

CASE STUDY 13.1: NATURE WORKSHOPS

Nature Workshops (www.natureworkshops.co.uk) is a Cornwall-based social enterprise, working to reconnect children and adults with the natural world. Through outdoors-focused classes, workshops, events and training sessions, people are encouraged to interact with their environment and to experience the physical, mental and social benefits of time spent outdoors. Nature Workshops' recent Forest School project took place in a community woodland in West Cornwall owned by The Wildlife Trusts, with participants attending one day a week for six weeks.

(Continued)

(Continued)

It was specifically designed to help build self-esteem and resilience, using immersive activities in natural spaces, for a total of 30 hours of contact time. Eight adults took part: two women and six men, each diagnosed with mental health issues, including schizophrenia, psychosis and depression. They were referred by their community psychiatric nurses as well as other local health professionals. The project had a retention rate of over 80 per cent and everyone who completed the six weeks also achieved a Level 1 Forest School certificate, despite the majority having had no previous formal qualifications.

The activities were iterative, participant-focused and included survival skills, cooking over a fire and reflective play. Those attending were also encouraged to take inspiration from the woods and try their hand at creative tasks: 'I carved a wooden spoon from some cherry wood, it's the sort of thing I wouldn't even have attempted before, but it was really good for me to sit down and make the best wooden spoon I could. I've still got it, it's in my kitchen!'

Using a set of well-being indicators and coded transcripts from interviews, research shows that participants as well as their referrers and Nature Workshops' staff all found the sessions not only aided in the development of practical and personal skills, but also helped people feel optimistic about their future and increased their feeling of closeness to the natural world. The health and well-being impact of the programme was measured using the Warwick-Edinburgh Mental Well-Being Scale, in addition to varied qualitative measures as part of a citizen science project funded by Plymouth University. Following the success of this project, Nature Workshops have since worked on several programmes in woodlands across Devon and Cornwall, targeting

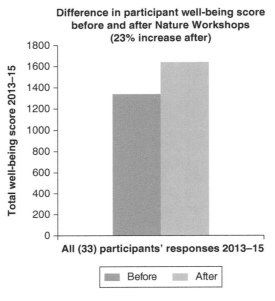

FIGURE 13.1 Well-being Scores

individuals with mental health problems, and have found a 23 per cent increase in well-being after attending one of their programmes (see Figure 13.1).

After taking part in one such project, one woman diagnosed with psychosis was able to come off her anti-psychotic drugs with the support of her GP. On speaking of the impact that the experience had on her, she said: 'I think it will probably last me all my life, quite frankly.' Another man, a 52-year-old struggling with social anxiety issues arising from long-term substance addiction, found the sessions helped increase his sense of self-worth. He said: 'It was about being confident but also respectful around other people and meeting challenges ... you know feeling part of a group cos during the thirty years in addiction I was always alone and the outsider.' He was referred to the programme as he was already volunteering on conservation and gardening projects. He had been out of work for some time but, after the course, now hopes to find employment: 'It was very empowering and left me with a very, very good feel for being out in the woods and for being around people ... I'm really glad I did it.'

Case Study 13.1 uses the 'Good from Woods' model described in Chapter 12 to record and evaluate their project. The results recorded are heart-warming but there is evidence from a variety of sources that all outdoor experiences increase mental health. For example, the mental health charity Mind lists seven therapeutic ways to be outdoors (Smith, 2015). It is important to reflect on what makes Forest School unique and consider the particular elements that make up a Forest School experience and how they relate to mental health needs. (The Forest School pedagogy diagram in Chapter 8, Figure 8.2, suggests headings to consider.)

Mitten (2009) describes 'the necessity of being in free nature and living with the natural rhythms of our earth' as essential elements in the healing power of nature. This speaks to the pedagogy of time, and, as the participants in Case Study 13.1 spent 5-hour days in the woods, the opportunities were there to follow the natural rhythms of the activities they participated in. Time is an important part of the Forest School experience but time is not unique to Forest School. It is equally possible to follow natural rhythms in a gardening project. The Therapeutic Landscapes Network (www.healingland-scapes.org/about/mission.html) is mostly concerned with linking adults to gardens, saving the wilder space for children, and gardening is undoubtedly therapeutic for many people.

Being in a wooded space is fundamental to Forest School, echoing Jung who perceived woods as places of deep meaning and spirituality (Jung, 1967: 86). His recognition of the importance of trees can be linked to his contributions on the generative powers of nature in therapy. Kardan et al. (2015) note the unique healing powers of trees but their research was conducted in an urban space. Nilsson and colleagues (2011: 3) attempted to make a clearer link, but the line between woods and other wild green spaces was still blurred. Perhaps it is more helpful to come to trees via the pedagogy of place, for, as Deakin says, 'To enter a wood is to pass into a different world in which we ourselves are transformed' (2008: x). Wattchow and Brown (2011: 72) discuss place as partly a cultural construct, partly a security need, partly a metaphysical experience. They propose a place-responsive pedagogy in outdoor education (ibid.: 180), and I would contend that Forest School is just that, using the power of trees to create a supportive place for healing and growth (as in both case studies described in this chapter).

What happens in these spaces is, of course, important, and Case Study 13.1 lists bushcraft activities common in all Forest School sessions such as cooking over a fire and making a wooden spoon. The Nature Workshops team elsewhere (Acton & Carter, 2016) describes these as 'immersive' activities – in other words, activities that are so absorbing and deeply involving that they take the participant to a different mental place, something adults can sometimes find it difficult to do, particularly when bound up with a depression or stressful life event. The attention restoration theory of Kaplan and Kaplan (1995) states that such absorbing contact with nature allows participants to relax and heal. The natural environment needs to have structure and to be one that the individual feels an infinity with. Forest School sessions have sufficient structure and, as we have discussed, create a sense of place. This is linked to the biophilia hypothesis that helps our understanding of why it is that contact with the natural world is necessary for mental health (Kellert & Wilson, 1993). This is the holding space that Forest School creates within the wooded environment where the trees, not the leaders, offer a therapeutic experience.

Herein lies the principle challenge to Forest School practitioners. Unless they have additional qualifications, they are not therapists. However, as a part of their training they will have encountered mindfulness as a technique to improve their capacity to be in the moment and to experience fully the environment they are in. They will have practised sharing those techniques with others. They will have been trained to reflect on their experiences at Forest School and to encourage others to do so, too. Greenaway and Knapp speak of the importance of 'connection before, during and after experiences' (2016: 267) in order to make meaning of our experiences. Cree and Gersie (2014: 62) link this process to Forest School. The sessions are unique in the combination of elements of place, time, nature, activities and reflective practices that meet the needs of these participants for restorative restoration. As Wattchow and Brown (2011: 196) advocate, practitioners are place-responsive and interact with participants to co-create the experiential learning.

This is not formal ecotherapy. The practitioners are not de facto trained as ecotherapists. Case Study 13.1 mentions the role of health professionals working alongside the participants. Forest School leaders are the facilitators and co-creators of the sessions, as they are in Case Study 13.2.

CASE STUDY 13.2: BOULDNOR FOREST CENTRE

The Hampshire and Isle of Wight Wildlife Trust leases the Bouldnor Forest Centre from the Forestry Commission (under licence for educational purposes) and uses it to deliver Forest School sessions to a wide range of groups, as well as a range of other wildlife and environmental activities. Kathy Grogan is the Education Officer for the Isle of Wight and is a trained Forest School leader. Although funding constraints are forcing her to scale back her offer, she still has some regular groups, three of which are of relevance here.

The first is a three-year project funded by the Blagrave Trust to deliver three 12-week Forest School programmes per year for disadvantaged youngsters of any age. This charity supports vulnerable and disadvantaged children and young people, chiefly in Hampshire and the Isle of Wight. We have discussed the benefits of such an opportunity for these young people, boosting their confidence, self-esteem and social skills.

The second is her Monday group for adults with mental health issues. This was funded for the initial three years by the National Health Service and then by the National Lottery through a Reaching Communities grant. Clients attend weekly sessions throughout the year. That they choose to do so speaks of the success they perceive arising from the sessions.

The third is a Thursday group for parents (or grandparents or carers) and toddlers called 'Wildlife Tots'. These are paid for either by session or by term by the adults in the group, and they are encouraged to repeat their visits to gain the benefits of Forest School.

Between the second and third groups, some interesting exchanges have developed out of community links and the site itself.

The site is on the Heritage Coast with Mesolithic and Palaeolithic remains in the shallow sea below the low cliff edge that is heavily eroded. There are the remains of a Second World War gun emplacement and associated buildings within stands of conifers that boast a large red squirrel population. Surrounding them, the replanting of native broadleaf trees is creating interesting glades, and Kathy has established base camps across the site as well as the main camp amongst the pines. There she has a mud kitchen as well as a fire circle and barbeque space, a digging area, and natural musical instruments hanging between the trees.

The sessions run as all Forest School sessions do. And as with all sessions it is the individuals that create the opportunities. A grandfather coming to the Thursday group is a retired archaeologist and he now adds his knowledge to the adult sessions, enabling them to widen the scope of their activities. He sees the intergenerational groups as replicating in some ways the groups of children, women and older people that would have existed in the Mesolithic and Palaeolithic communities when the hunters were away. One of the mental health clients has gained enough resilience from the Monday session to bring her niece to the Thursday session, and a grandpa who attended on Thursday is now benefitting from coming on Monday, too, gaining

(Continued)

(Continued)

enough confidence to become a core volunteer at both groups. Around 100 families come to the Thursday group, fortunately not all at once. Many of the younger adults are not confident in wild spaces. They are using Forest School to gain confidence to share these spaces with their children. Many of the older adults are helping to share their skills and gaining needed social interactions.

The Monday group of participants, described in Case Study 13.2, can engage with the sessions as much or as little as they feel able to, progressing from drinking tea that has been made for them by the campfire to initiating environmental projects, such as tree planting, themselves. The sessions start with attention being given to the establishment of their sense of security, creating within them a sense of place. From there, they are given time to develop their sense of agency, moving at their own speed, from waiting to be offered a drink by the fire to making it themselves when they want one. They can then develop their confidence and self-esteem by engaging with bushcraft and environmental tasks to sustain the site and themselves. This is not a formalised ecotherapy – the Forest School leaders do not presume to have the skills to take on a therapeutic role – but the trees do have that therapeutic effect. This is ecotherapy by proxy, and leaders need to be aware of their limitations as well as of their offer, and be prepared to say no when the challenges are beyond their competence.

However, the effectiveness of the sessions in Case Study 13.2 is measurable in two ways. One is in the links between the Thursday and the Monday sessions, as hitherto fragile individuals become part of a community. The other is that participants elect to use their personal health budgets to pay to attend the sessions, indicating that their perception is that the sessions are effective. As Burls (2007) identifies, all ecotherapies are more effective when service users assume greater responsibility towards personal behaviour change. Burls also links ecotherapy to sustainability: 'for sustainable therapy and recovery, sustainable public mental health and sustainable healthy public green spaces' (ibid.: 37).

These are just two examples of a growing trend towards Forest School sessions for adults with mental health problems. They clearly have beneficial effects and speak to a need for a connection with a wooded environment. However, if the trend becomes a flood, then Forest School leaders may need to reflect carefully on two issues. One is whether they are competent to deal with all the issues being presented to them or whether they need additional training, in counselling for example. The other is whether there is a danger of agencies seeing Forest School as a cheap alternative to deeper psychotherapeutic sessions. Both of these issues have ethical implications for

OTHER FOREST SCHOOL OCCURRENCES

practitioners. The FSA Code of Conduct (www.forestschoolassociation.org/members-code-of-conduct/) requires practitioners to develop ethical practices, but, as yet, has not specified what these should be.

GOING FORWARD

REFLECTIONS ON FOREST SCHOOL

This chapter raises the question of whether Forest School is a pedagogy, i.e. a way of teaching, or a therapy, as in a way of remediating health problems, or neither of these or both. From the earliest research, it has been apparent that Forest School improves well-being and concentration on learning. Practitioners are trained in emotional intelligence and in how people learn. It is important for practitioners to reflect on the 'placing' of Forest School and how that informs their practice. In particular, it requires practitioners to reflect on their own code of ethics. Reflect on the ethics of Forest School as a therapy and what that could mean for leaders' training needs.

IDEAS FOR PRACTICE: SPOON MAKING (FIGURE 13.2)

One of the participants in Case Study 13.1 mentions the satisfaction derived from making a useable spoon, and this would therefore seem like a good idea to focus on. Wooden spoons come in all forms of complexity, from Welsh love spoons to everyday kitchen utensils. At the basic level, they do not have to be hard to make, and, indeed, if they end up looking more like a spatula than a spoon, it really doesn't matter.

There are essentially three stages: preparing a blank, roughing out the blank and finishing off the carving. Once you have a blank, it is possible to work with just two tools – a small axe and a knife – and a chopping block. You can just use a plain straight whittling knife or you can also use a hook knife to shape the bowl. There are websites devoted to spoon carving and, indeed, there is an annual festival in August in the UK where you can go and compare your efforts with the experts and learn some new techniques (see http://spoonfest.co.uk/whats-on/).

Preparing a blank is similar to sawing the discs described in the Ideas for Practice at the end of Chapter 5, just longer. You need a piece of green wood that is about the length you want the spoon to be. In Case Study 13.1, they used cherry wood but sycamore is a nice pale wood with a straight grain, and plentiful. The straighter the grain, the easier it will be. Pine is a soft wood; that makes life easier, too, although it may taint food with its resin. Alder is a good wood to start with, as are both apple and birch. Go online for further ideas.

FIGURE 13.2   Spoon or Spatula

Once you have a log of the right length, you need to split it in two lengthways. If you place the axe carefully on the centre of the top of the log and hit it with a wooden mallet, you should split the log in half. Don't hit it with a metal mallet, as you risk sparks and such. Decide which end is the bowl and which the handle and put notches in the split log about where the back of the bowl will start. This allows you to use the axe to strip the bark off the back of the log without wrecking the curve of the bowl – you can do that later! Once all the bark has been removed from both ends, you have a spoon blank. On the flat surface, using a fat pen, draw your spoon – roughly. It won't end up looking like that.

The next step is to follow the outline and roughly shape the spoon. This is usually done with an axe but if the spoon is very small you could just use a knife. If you use the axe, you can make 'stopping cuts' with a saw to protect the bowl end. Watch where your non-axe hand is and where the axe will go if (when) it slips. When you decide to move from axe to knife is personal choice – the knife makes slower but more controllable progress.

You are now whittling away until you are happy that you have created the spoon of your choice. Always remember to work with the blade of the knife facing away from your body and be conscious of where it will go if (when) it slips.

FURTHER READING

- The Nature Workshops team involved in Case Study 13.1 has published an article on a similar project that is an informative read: Acton, J. & Carter, B. (2016) 'The impact of immersive outdoor activities in local woodlands on young carers' emotional literacy and well-being', *Comprehensive Child and Adolescent Nursing*, 1–3.
- There are a number of interesting articles available by clicking on the link below; the one listed here is the one cited in the chapter: Mitten, D. (2009) 'The healing power of nature: the need for nature for human health, development, and wellbeing', paper presented at Ibsen: Friluftsliv Jubilee Conference, Levanger, Norway, 14–19 September. Available at http://norwegianjournaloffriluftsliv.com/doc/122010.pdf
- A simple guide to the different types of ecotherapies for the lay reader is available from Mind, the leading UK mental health charity: Smith, J. (2015) *Making Sense of Ecotherapy*. London: Mind.
- A more academic consideration of ecotherapy is this article: Burls, A. (2007) 'People and green spaces: promoting public health and mental well-being through ecotherapy', *Journal of Public Mental Health*, 6(3): 24–38.
- Reflecting on the ethical codes of allied therapies is helpful when considering what is important for Forest School – for example, that of the play therapists: Dighton, R. (2008) *An Ethical Basis for Good Practice in Play Therapy*. Weybridge: British Association of Play Therapists.

14

Supporting Parents

All the independent practitioners and charities mentioned in this book are now offering Forest School sessions to families. With the help of two case studies, this chapter will consider why that might be, what lessons we can draw and what it tells us about parents' perceptions of their relationship with nature. It will also consider what this could mean for future developments in Forest School.

CASE STUDY 14.1: URBAN FOREST SCHOOL FOR FAMILIES – IMPRESSIONS FROM TEN SESSIONS LED BY AN EXPERIENCED PRACTITIONER AND SUPPORTED BY NURSERY STAFF FROM CHILDREN'S CENTRES IN BERMONDSEY, SOUTH LONDON

Written by Rich Sylvester (Forest School trainer and story teller)

Each week, we travel a mile across the innercity with a group of 2- and 3-year-old children and their parent or carer. Our Forest Fun site is a carefully chosen grassy area with mature trees and a chalk stream flowing from a small waterfall. The waterfall, shallow pool and stepping stones are a magnet for the children dressed in their waterproofs and boots. Initially, some walk into the water and jump, whilst

(Continued)

(Continued)

others stand at the edge wondering, looking and listening. As the sessions evolve, they follow their leaf boats downstream, throw gravel into the water, 'fish' with little sticks and string. Some children splash and jump together in shared excitement. We see them move to help each other up when they fall. 'You must do something different next week or we will never get them out of the water' (nursery staff after Session 1). We agree that it is valuable for children to repeat their experiences and that this chance to do so is much reduced after they enter primary education.

Fears of 'dirt' (mud) are strong and I reassure parents that the 'dirty water' is actually from a pure chalk aquifer, deep underground. In evaluation, several parents reflected on how they overcame their fears during the sessions (e.g. snails, worms, the 'creepy forest'). By the end, all parents reflected on the positive experience: 'Enjoyment of natural quiet environment (bird sounds, trees, water, etc.) brought back past memories of youthful age, confidence and learning for my daughter, exploring.'

Away from the water, I leave a long cotton rope, a camouflage net, a basket of pine cones, small buckets, some natural clay and a bag of sticks. The children chose to play with these at different times, often joined by the adults: 'I am playing with my child like I was a child.' There are moments sitting together around snack time when the adults start to create rhythms with sticks and sing songs from their childhood: 'The forest nature brings back old memories for our parents, but good memories. Some were able to talk about their past and how they played outside' (nursery staff).

Later, we rig a hammock and also parallel ropes to climb on with hands and feet. Some children find these and start to test themselves on the ropes, balancing and falling, with an adult nearby to ensure safety. Others need a little help to get into the hammock but, once there, they are reluctant to abandon their gentle rocking.

Case Study 14.1 records impressions from sessions where parents have been encouraged to take their children outside by nursery staff. Key to these impressions is noting the transition for both nursery workers and parents from fear to positivity. The nursery workers were initially fearful that the children would 'waste' the sessions playing in the water, whilst the parents were fearful of elements in the environment that they perceived as dangers. The staff came to appreciate a more child-led approach and the parents came to value and remember their childhood experiences of the outdoors. This echoes the report of family Forest School on Merseyside (Ridgers & Sayers, 2010), which found that sessions such as these increased family participation in natural outdoor play opportunities, as they helped families to overcome the barriers they felt existed to their participation in natural play. In this study, it was also notable that the majority of parents reported greater freedom in their own play opportunities and in the distance that they had roamed from home as children, and they often stated that they were lucky to have this freedom. In some cases, parents lamented how different their play was to their children's and the impact that restrictions on children may have. The adults' freedom in their play opportunities as children indicates that they were enabled to engage in natural play and that this had been reinforced by their parents (Ridgers & Sayers, 2010).

Research has shown that it is the family environment that is a key determinant of natural play engagement and opportunities (Sallis & Owen, 2002). However, it is not always possible to persuade parents outside, as the Bradford West project found: 'The original plan had been to involve parents and their children in the sessions but the weather put off all but one of the parents' (Horseman & Scott, 2010). Parents and adults generally are far more cautious about venturing out in what they perceive to be inclement weather than children are, which can create an obstacle to promoting outdoor learning in all settings. What is clear is that in Case Study 14.1 the Children's Centre workers had a strong enough relationship with the parents to encourage them outside, and having done so the parents then appreciated and valued their experience. The first lesson to draw from these different examples is that for natural play to return as a normal part of children's growing up, their parents have to be supported in the decision-making process to join their children outside. Trusting the adults who are doing the encouraging is important.

This is an echo of the work of Partridge and Taylor (2011), who were able to use their existing relationship with families to encourage them out into the woods. The project was to help vulnerable parents to learn to play and interact with their children using the medium of Forest School and the outcomes were very positive (ibid.: 205), with 88 per cent of parents feeling more confident about participating in outdoor activities with their children. Similarly, Horseman and Scott (2010) were able to show benefits to the children and to the staff, but where the parents were also brought on board the incentive to go outside became embedded in the family culture. This is demonstrated in Case Study 14.2, where parents have elected to sign up for Forest School sessions for a variety of reasons. The second lesson to draw from these examples is that if parents come out to Forest School sessions, then they enjoy the experience and can appreciate their value.

CASE STUDY 14.2: RURAL FOREST SCHOOL FOR FAMILIES

Holly Hilder is an independent Forest School practitioner working on the Suffolk–Essex border. As well as going out to settings to run sessions, she also uses the Daws Hall Nature Reserve which has been an environmental resource for over 50 years. The reserve has woodland, wildflower meadows and a stream amongst its habitats. Holly runs family sessions both in term-time for families with very young children and in the school holidays for whole families. These latter sessions are not, strictly speaking, Forest School as they are less than six sessions, but they build on the sessions for little ones and offer opportunities for working parents to join the group. Holly calls her sessions 'Family Forest Fun'.

On a July day in 2015, 12 families with children from babes-in-arms to older primary spent a relaxed morning with Holly and her partner. There were at least four dads. Some of the families were new to Forest School but most were not. Some were from the term-time group, bringing siblings who felt they had been missing out. Some had been as pre-schoolers but now attended schools that don't offer it to older children and some were from playgroups that don't do it. The children shared the basic rules with each other as did the parents. While they waited for everyone to assemble and register, several children climbed trees. Then the session started with a walk through wildflower meadow, catching bugs and butterflies en route. When we reached the stream, we stopped to dip nets and race cork boats, paddle and search for crayfish (see Figure 14.1). The children knew what they wanted to do and where to find the materials to create the boats, etc. The bigger children (some of the adults) clearly enjoyed being led into the established games and activities.

Then the leaders encouraged the group to climb up into the wood to the fire site (see Figure 14.2). Once again, the children led the way, keen to share the excitement with new adults and children. They could choose to engage with fire lighting, making clay objects, balancing on ropes, making bracelets, creating mud faces on trees, or cooking – toasting marshmallow and making pancake balls. Or some just played together in the wood. Most parents found security in the structured activities, whilst many children did not. Here are some of their comments:

'I'm enjoying this, I think he is.'

'This is for me, she gets it in term time and I'm so envious.'

'They just love it so much, it's what they should be doing.'

'The schools don't do it after reception/Year 1.' (This from three parents)

'We could do this at home, but we don't, so coming here ensures it happens.'

'We brought the whole preschool in a coach, and it was so good, I had to come back with the girls. They only have a tiny copse at the preschool and they can't light fires.'

'My neighbour asked us to come with them, and it's great.'

OTHER FOREST SCHOOL OCCURRENCES

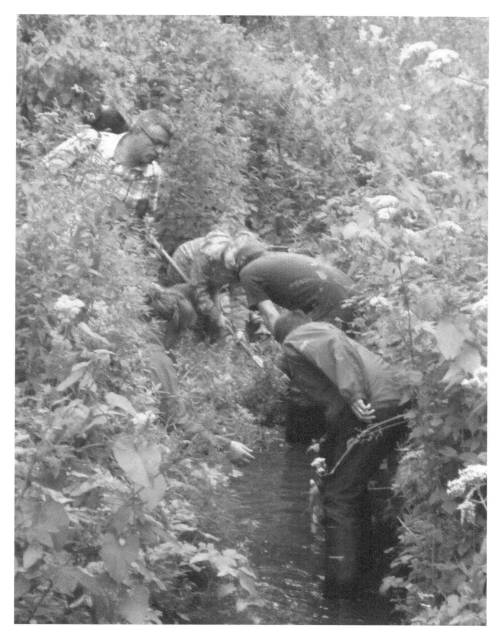

FIGURE 14.1   Children of All Ages in the Stream

My impression is that with these sessions, Holly is embedding Forest School into the community and supporting the parents by sharing skills and building their confidence.

(Continued)

(Continued)

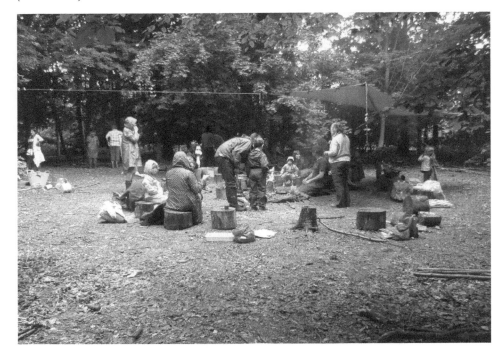

FIGURE 14.2   Family Forest Fun

Most of the parents in Case Study 14.2 had already 'bought into' the benefits of Forest School and natural play. What seems to be stopping them from going out on their own is their confidence levels about what to do and how to do it. The practitioners are modelling ways to be outside and demonstrating that it is not necessary to be like the adventurer Bear Grylls to have a meaningful and exciting outing to a wild space. This echoes my own experience with groups of students of all ages and abilities. What is missing, what is stopping them from taking their own children outside both as parents and as practitioners, are two elements.

The first is the adults' own direct experience of outdoor spaces. Too many adults in the UK today have had limited experience of undirected outdoor play. Three words: undirected, outdoor and play. By undirected activities, I mean those freely chosen without prompts from an authority figure. To be able to undertake these, the participant needs to be sufficiently self-aware and confident to decide what it is that they want to do and then how to go about it. In his influential report, Gill (2007: 12) charts the 'shrinking freedom of action' in children's worlds from the 1970s to 2006, when he carried out his research. The children experiencing those losses are the parents of today, and too often their capacity for undirected action has been constrained by the limitations placed on them as children, particularly in respect of outdoor experiences. And play – an intrinsically motivated, freely chosen, personally directed process (Else, 2009: 11) – is not seen for what it is, namely what it is that humans normally and naturally do to find out about themselves and the world around them (ibid.: 30). It is no wonder that these parents value the support of the Forest School practitioner in the woods. The lesson to learn here is that parents need their own direct experiences upon which to base their activities with their children.

The second and related element that stops adults taking children outside is fear of risk. In the period described by Gill, 1970–2006, 'risk' became a negative association with primarily physical activities, often in outdoor spaces, so entrenched in popular culture in the UK that the Health and Safety Executive (HSE) felt it necessary to issue a statement in 2012 encouraging reasonable risks (HSE, 2012). This negative mindset still leaves many of the parents of today fearful of the outdoors and unable to direct their own activities without an authority figure to support them. The lesson here is that parents need support in terms of both knowledge and confidence to manage reasonable risks.

In 2007, UNICEF published a study of children's well-being that placed Britain at the bottom of the league of the 21 richest countries. By 2013, when the study was done again, we had climbed to 16 out of 29 (UNICEF UK, 2013). Better but not brilliant. UNICEF has passed the baton on to the Jacob's Foundation for the 2015 survey published in 2016. Its survey of 8-year-olds in 16 countries puts England at 13 in questions about 'life as a whole' (Rees et al., 2016). Fearfulness, lack of agency and separation from nature must play a part in creating these dreadful statistics. This lesson is that, in the UK, we are missing at least one generation of parents who have played outdoors, and this has had an impact on the well-being of the next generation.

In the USA, the response to Richard Louv's 2009 book has been the founding of the Children and Nature Network (www.childrenandnature.org/about/), which engages parents as well as others to 'reconnect children with nature'. I struggle with the word 'reconnect' – the children they are working with have never had the chance to connect, so they can't reconnect. Some of the adults can because they did, but for everyone else it is 'connect', something new. The website is full of ideas but some do reflect a culture where close supervision and adult controls are the norm. In the UK, the film *Project Wild Thing* was launched in 2013 and led to the foundation of The Wild Network (www.thewildnetwork.com/), also largely parent-led, with a 'vision to re-wild childhood, grow Wild Time (time outside) and help kids thrive in the 21st century'. These grass-roots movements indicate that parents are recognising nature deficit as a phenomenon that needs addressing, and some of them are coming to Forest School sessions as one way of acquiring the outdoor skills and experiences they need.

This feels like a positive way forward, both for Forest School and for parents, as a way to create a more sustainable future for our children. Forest School practitioners can develop opportunities for families to create a shared confidence in engaging playfully with nature, rather than using nature as a commodity on which to impose human technology. The unique selling point (USP) for Forest School is in the specialised nature of the engagement offered to parents, of being centred on their individual needs but always interwoven with 'the ever-changing moods and marvels, potential and challenges of the natural world through the seasons to fill every Forest School session and programme with discovery and difference' (FSA, 2016b). If the engagements are natural and playful, then they are more likely to be deeply engaging (immersive), and another platform for sustainability will be created.

GOING FORWARD

REFLECTIONS ON FOREST SCHOOL

A juggling act for leaders is how to meet the needs of both parents and children and still allow both groups the space to determine and lead their own activities. At Forest School, each individual participant is:

- equal, unique and valuable
- competent to explore and discover
- entitled to experience appropriate risk and challenge
- entitled to choose, and to initiate and drive their own learning and development
- entitled to experience regular success
- entitled to develop positive relationships with themselves and other people
- entitled to develop a strong, positive relationship with their natural world. (FSA, 2016b)

There are a variety of ways to do this, from having two sets of leaders, one dealing primarily with the children and one with the adults, to having enough space for the group to divide into self-determining subgroups, as is the case in Case Study 14.2. Reflect on what some issues may be where you have adults and children in the same group and each with their own play needs.

IDEAS FOR PRACTICE: MUSICAL INSTRUMENTS

It is possible to make sounds in a variety of ways in the woods and once participants have a sound-making option, they can enhance story-telling and song sessions, or just improvise natural music. Here are some starting points for ideas for musical instruments:

1   Percussive sounds are the easiest. Logs of different sizes and density (the result of decay) will create different pitches and volumes. A row of poles stuck upright in the ground can have sticks run across them like a xylophone. Old pots make a variation on wood sounds.

2   Bullroarers date back to paleolithic times and occur in all ancient cultures, so they are not hard to make. The downside is that spinning a piece of wood in the air requires a good-sized and empty clearing! Start off in the same way as for a spoon but once the log is spilt, split it again to give you a thin slice from the centre of the log. Shape the ends to a pleasing curve and make a hole in one end. It can be decorated, too. You will need strong but thin cord with a loop at one end so that you can swing it around your head – the sound that is created is low but carries long distances.

3   Whistles should be easy but I haven't got the knack. The idea is to remove the soft pith from elder wood, which is easy enough. Plug one end up (or don't remove all the pith) and make a notch about 3 cm from the open end with a perpendicular cut at the open end and a 45-degree cut towards it. The tricky bit for me has always been the last step, which is to find a piece of wood that will fit into the open end, shave one side to make it flat, and jam it in the open end. Good luck. I have more success with panpipes, binding different lengths of hollowed elder together and blowing across the top – at least I get a sound with those! And wind chimes are even easier as the lengths are just suspended so that they hit each other in the wind.

4   Aolian harps is the name for instruments that are played by the wind crossing taut strings – if you have a spare bucket you can thread the string through and you will amplify the sound – it is subtle and mysterious. Experiment – it's great fun.

FURTHER READING

- Look at the websites of the two parent-led organisations and consider what they tell you about the fears and concerns that are common to both and look for the cultural differences between them: The Wild Network (www.thewildnetwork.com/) and The Children and Nature Network (www.childrenandnature.org/).

(Continued)

- Read at least one of the other case studies mentioned in the chapter and compare them with the case studies in the following two texts. What are the similarities and are there any significant differences to think about? Partridge, L. & Taylor, W. (2011) 'Forest school for families', in Knight, S. (ed.) *Forest School for All.* London: Sage; and Ridgers, N. & Sayers, J. (2010) *Natural Play in the Forest: Forest School Evaluation.* London: Natural England.
- Play is just so important to human health, and Perry Else has explained it so well in his book: Else, P. (2009) *The Value of Play.* London: Continuum.
- Tim Gill's report has been very influential so it is a must, and it is a free download! Gill, T. (2007) *No Fear: Growing Up in a Risk Averse Society.* London: Caloustie Gulbenkian Foundation.

15

Holistic Perspectives and Conclusions

In this book, I have argued that Forest School has a beneficial role in the UK, supporting development, learning and mental health. Having considered how Forest School is being delivered across age groups and geographies and some of the benefits that have been recorded, it is time to step back and consider the bigger picture. For example, if the diversity of groups accessing Forest School as described continues, what are the implications for training and what could the role of the Forest School Association be? What implications are there for the sustainability agenda and what could governmental recognition look like? Lastly, the conclusion will consider existing and possible future international links, given the existence of Forest School and similar activities across Northern Europe and the development already of Forest Kindergarten in South Korea, Bush Kindergarten in Australia and Forest School in Canada.

When considering the diversity of groups accessing Forest School sessions, it is useful to summarise the similarities and consistencies as well as the differences. On interrogating the various deliveries using the pedagogy model (Figure 8.2) in Chapter 8, I have shown that all Forest School groups are similar in that they all follow the same pattern, establishing over a number of sessions a level of trust between leaders and participants that enables a client-led approach, and challenges that promote the growth of confidence, well-being and social interactions. The approach allows for the 'uncertainty, agency, authenticity and mastery' (Beames & Brown, 2016: 6) demanded of adventurous outdoor learning. In Chapter 3, I discussed the relevance of Forest School to brain development and returned to that theme in Chapter 12. Behavioural change is reflected in changes in the brain, and, as participants get older, these changes take longer to achieve, hence the importance of Forest School over time. These consistencies make Forest School a reliable approach for clients to access.

The differences that have been considered are in part practical. Funders and clients are willing to commission only just so many sessions initially and some practitioners are more persuasive than others in obtaining the maximum number of sessions affordable. For example, 'Into the Woods' in the Bristol area is doing fantastic work with adults with learning difficulties, but typically is booked for six-week blocks only (https://intothewoodsuk. wordpress.com/). It is to be hoped that as the benefits become more widely recognised, not only will potential clients be more aware of the need for longer blocks of sessions, but also the practitioners will feel more able to negotiate longer contracts. Not doing so will undermine the reliability of the outcomes identified above.

Some differences are ideological, particularly in early years groups, as described in Part 1. In some nature kindergartens, the children are out all day rather than just for half a day a week, and there are also different ways of working outdoors in the early years that need clearer differentiation, as they all have importance and a role to play in promoting the healthy development of young children. But Forest School has always been a broad church and attending to the principles of good practice, as outlined by the Forest School Association (FSA, 2011), enables practitioners to assure themselves that they can pursue their own ideology under the Forest School umbrella, provided that these criteria are met.

A greater challenge for Forest School practitioners is in embracing the benefits of Forest School as an eco-therapy without committing themselves beyond their competence. The groups described in this book are clearly working effectively and clients are being monitored by health professionals where appropriate. Sempik et al. (2010: 22) describe the breadth of scope of 'green care' as including important non-health professionals. However, there is a need to acknowledge a potential risk and to develop a code of ethics to cover any expansion of the purview of Forest School leaders into therapeutic roles, where they do not have the necessary additional training.

A difference to be celebrated is the greater role of Forest School in working with families and adults who have come to Forest School as a recognition of the benefits to the wider population of a close relationship with the natural world. An organisation that exemplifies this range of activities is Forest School Swansea Neath Port Talbot, described in Case Study 15.1.

CASE STUDY 15.1: FOREST SCHOOL SWANSEA NEATH PORT TALBOT

Forest School Swansea Neath Port Talbot (www.forestschoolsnpt.org.uk/) was set up in 2001 as a charity and company limited by guarantee to provide Forest School opportunities for children and young people across the south of Wales from Swansea and Neath to Port Talbot. It has six part-time staff, a team of trained leaders and assistants employed on a sessional basis and a pool of volunteers who run Forest School sessions for all ages, plus training, consultancy and awareness sessions, children's parties and corporate events. The key for the calendar (see Figure 15.1) says it all!

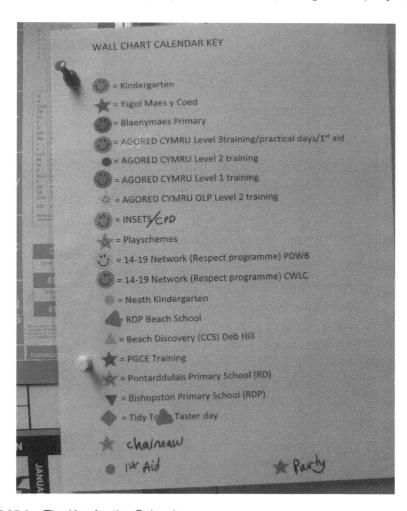

FIGURE 15.1   The Key for the Calendar

(Continued)

(Continued)

The regular parent and toddler group in Bishop's Wood on the outskirts of Swansea is so popular that, in 2016, it expanded to two sessions a week in term time. To maintain the ethos of the sessions, numbers are limited to 12 families per session, usually with just one parent attending. On the day I visited, there were four dads and five mums plus two non-parent carers. The staff included a trustee of the charity and two volunteer teenagers on work experience. The site is well away from the road along a valley path and has a turf-roofed shelter with a fire pit and trails leading off into more dense woodland; one group set off in search of dinosaurs. Children explored, engaged with typical Forest School activities and played together, while the adults shared ideas, gained confidence and appreciated their local environment (see Figure 15.2). The group shared a warm drink and a snack midway through the session, lighting a fire as a focal point, even in summer.

Through sessions such as these, the charity aims to encourage everyone to respect and actively care for their local natural environment so that they will appreciate the green spaces on their doorsteps and let future generations have those same experiences. They want all children and young people to have the chance to be able to look back on their childhood with magical memories of playing in the woods, getting muddy, discovering bugs and eating food cooked on the fire that they made.

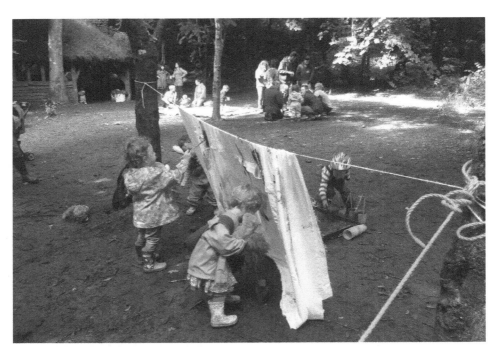

FIGURE 15.2   A Forest School Community

This case study is typical of many independent Forest School organisations and demonstrates how Forest School is fulfilling a societal need, described by Öhman and Sandell (2016: 32) as 'nature as fosterer' – in other words, nature as a vital element of experiences that link people and nature. Öhman and Sandell reinforce the idea that 'personal landscape relationships give human ecological references to people's dependence on the environment' (ibid.: 38), illustrating that such nature–human relationships are essential for a sustainable future. The cognitive dissonance that is felt when individuals feel the importance of their connectedness to nature, but at the same time a separateness from it, was one of the findings of Vinning et al. (2008). They also suggest that resolving this conflict through enabling closer relationships with nature should lead to more environmentally responsible behaviour. This is the role that Forest School for families is fulfilling.

These studies are not specific to woods but this book is. I have referenced the importance of trees to the human psyche, citing Jung amongst others as a justification. Certainly, if one accepts the importance of 'place', then the siting of a base camp in a clearing surrounded by trees makes that connection stronger still, as the site is easily identified as a central focal point, a 'place'. And trees hold the element of time in their branches; Deakin (2008: 384) spoke of trees lasting 200 and 500 years that give us a sense of ecological continuity. A 2013 report for Woodlands.co.uk (Leach, 2013) is entitled 'Happiness Grows on Trees', and pulls together the results of studies indicating the benefits of wooded spaces in particular, as well as adding some new research into the effects of woods on well adults. Enabling more people to feel that they can access woods will be good for the health of the populace and good for the health of the environment.

Many of the studies cited in this book have been qualitative in nature. This is inevitable and a growing trend in the social sciences. The comparative value of such studies has been discussed in Sempik et al. (2010: 114) and, as they recommend, the research group of the FSA is encouraging the continuing recording and monitoring of projects to amass a body of evidence that can be interrogated by academics (www.forestschoolassociation.org/forum-index/forum-index/general/research-into-forest-school-practice/), as is the Good from Woods project (https://goodfromwoods.wordpress.com/the-tool-kit/). This enables a blending of practitioners' commitment to recording projects with the academic rigour necessary to study their findings.

As the outcomes from various projects are recorded and discussed, so the issue of increasing the levels of and access to training is rising up the agenda in many colleges and universities in the UK. This is not about well-established routes into the more traditional forms of outdoor education, such as climbing and canoeing, but rather about the embedding of the importance of outdoor learning into the culture of general teacher training and early years education. Making the outdoors a normal place to be and to learn in is essential for recognising its universal importance. Case Study 15.2 of the work at Cardiff Metropolitan University is an example of how this is beginning to happen.

CASE STUDY 15.2: CARDIFF METROPOLITAN UNIVERSITY

Chantelle Haughton is a senior lecturer in the School of Education at Cardiff Metropolitan University and, like four of her colleagues, is a Level 3 Forest School practitioner. On the Cyncoed campus where they work is the Outdoor Learning Centre hub for learning and research, a 7-metre-wide circular classroom providing a comfortable learning environment, all in the surroundings of a small strip of ancient woodland complete with other forest-based learning spaces such as three log circles and a yurt, and all on the same campus. Within the BA (Hons) Early Childhood Studies course, they deliver modules on the benefits and challenges of outdoor play and learning, which include practical activities in the woodland and Outdoor Learning Centre, and which offer the opportunity to gain an accredited Forest School Level 1 qualification as well as being a part of undergraduate programmes. Level 3 Forest School training is provided for local teachers and practitioners.

A range of outdoor learning, play and Forest School projects which run at Cyncoed campus are designed to promote social inclusion, learning and development through community cohesion and are coordinated by Chantelle. Undergraduate student volunteers help the Outdoor Learning team to provide different woodland activities throughout the year for local children and practitioners. These ongoing bespoke projects may be run on a weekly, termly or annual basis and involve practitioners, pupils and parents from local primary schools, secondary schools, health care settings, home education groups, Play Wales and local Community First areas.

Lee Thomas, head teacher at Meadowlane Primary School, says:

'Pupils and staff love to visit Queens Wood to work within this rich learning landscape. These projects provide an exciting and unique development opportunity for children and practitioners. It's also significant in nurturing positive attitudes towards lifelong learning that our pupils experience an encouraging connection with a local Higher Education setting.'

Beth Warwick, Inclusion Manager at Lakeside Primary School, says:

'A group of pupils from Year 3 to Year 6 and class teacher Nic Rhodes visit campus each week for an after school club to take part in outdoor activities. Led by Chantelle and supported by a committed group of student volunteers, the pupils develop their social and emotional skills in a fun and relaxed environment. The children taking part in this club have shown a great improvement in confidence and communication skills over a short space of time – what a great opportunity! We are within walking distance of the university and so we are delighted to be working with the Outdoor Learning Team; a number of projects are ongoing involving pupils of different ages and their families.'

Chantelle's message is that:

'playing outdoors contributes to the wellbeing and resilience of human beings – particularly young ones. Having welcoming places, enough time and the company of others to play with, is of great consequence to all children and young people. As adults and practitioners we need to foster play and learning environments that support this.'

Whilst it is unusual to find four trained Forest School leaders on the staff, Cardiff Metropolitan is not alone in developing modules and opportunities for students to learn the benefits of outdoor learning experientially, and particularly on early years courses and early primary teacher training it is Forest School that is being used as the example. As we have seen, this is being embraced in Scotland and Wales at a state curriculum level. In these countries, a recognition of the need for outdoor experiential learning is being actively encouraged.

I have stated in Chapter 9 that it behoves all of us involved in education to construct our own philosophical stance about what the purpose of education is. For me, and in broad terms, it has to be about sustainability, at the level of the individual, at the level of society and at the widest planetary level. If I am right, then ensuring an engagement with nature at a cultural level is essential to the well-being of the individual and thus up to the well-being of the planet. Unhappy people cannot care about the planet if they do not care about themselves. One can argue with some justification that Forest School also sits in the disciplines of health and social care, and, if so, then it is time that the qualifications necessary to run some sessions are revisited and that a more formal code of ethics is adopted. For the health and well-being of the average person in the UK, we also have to make a cultural shift towards embracing something like the Scandinavian 'friluftsliv', still a core belief in the societies of the far north of Europe (Gurholt, 2016: 290). All forms of outdoor engagement have their place in such a cultural shift, but, as a starting point, Forest School offers supported opportunities to all ages and abilities, helping them to feel a sense of kinship with a place and a community.

GOING FORWARD

REFLECTIONS ON FOREST SCHOOL

Forest School has links to the outdoor kindergarten in Scandinavia and Germany, and together they have influenced developments across Northern Europe. Canada and Australia have developed their own Forest School and Bush School movements, respectively. Interestingly, South Korea, Japan and Singapore are developing Forest Kindergarten as a way of building the resilience of children before they tackle the rigours of formal schooling. It would be sad if it is the increasing formalisation and the dominance of a testing culture in English schools that creates the curriculum space for Forest School. Each country has shaded its offering with its own cultural differences, as is only appropriate, but has largely held to the Forest School principles that we would recognise. What can such a widespread interest tell us? Is this a recognition that all humans have the same fundamental needs, and, if so, what are they? Further research into cultural similarities and differences could reveal useful fundamental requirements for personal well-being through natural experiences, particularly for young children.

IDEAS FOR PRACTICE: NATURAL ART

From the earliest records, we can see that as a species we have a desire to create and record through art our responses to the natural world. Self-expression in the woods does not require great artistic prowess but can support the reflections and connections of an individual. Figures 15.3–15.6 show a progression from completely found to completely created, and are all works made by primary school children.

Figure 15.3 was a spotted spiral of fungi that was photographed as a natural work of art. Figure 15.4 was found lying down and its potential was spotted. Turned upside

FIGURE 15.3   Found Fungii

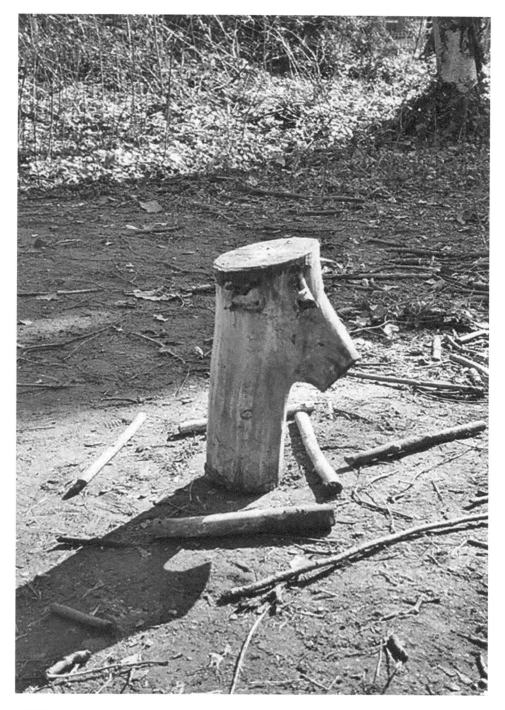

FIGURE 15.4   Found Stump

(Continued)

(Continued)

FIGURE 15.5   Making a Horse Head

FIGURE 15.6   A Grass Bug

down and framed with sticks it is a horse's head. Figure 15.5 is another horse's head but here the frame came first, then the triangular piece of bark was placed in the centre. After some contemplation, the rest of the picture was collected and constructed.

Figure 15.6 was the result of an intentional plan to create a grass bug that might be living in the wood alongside the children. All ages enjoy these kinds of activities. If you have not tried them, go out and see what you can find.

FURTHER READING

- Read the study by Vinning et al., to consider the cognitive dissonance between simultaneously feeling part of nature and not part of nature: Vinning, J., Merrick, M. & Price, E. (2008) 'The distinction between humans and nature: human perceptions of connectedness to nature and elements of the natural and unnatural', *Human Ecology Review*, 15(1): 1–11.
- This is an easy-to-read report on the benefit of being in the woods: Leach, J. (2013) 'Happiness Grows on Trees: How Woodlands Boost our Wellbeing'. Available at www.woodlands.co.uk/Woodlands.co.uk-HappinessGrowsOn-Trees-Feb13.pdf
- This is a less-easy read but more academic in nature, and pulls together different ways to experience green care: Sempik, J., Hine, R. & Wilcox, D. (2010) 'Green Care: A Conceptual Framework – A Report of the Working Group on the Health Benefits of Green Care'. COST Action 866, Green Care in Agriculture. Loughborough: Centre for Child and Family Research, Loughborough University.
- To viscerally appreciate connecting with nature, read 'Hidden Woods' – a poem by Hollie McNish. Better still, listen to her read the poem on YouTube: www.youtube.com/watch?v=6BhS6uuogkl or see the video on the Hidden Woods home page: www.hiddenwoods.co.uk

References

Acton, J. & Carter, B. (2016) 'The impact of immersive outdoor activities in local woodlands on young carers' emotional literacy and well-being', *Comprehensive Child and Adolescent Nursing*, 1–3.

Alexander, R. (ed.) (2010) *Children, their World, their Education: Final Report and Recommendations of the Cambridge Primary Review*. London: Routledge.

Allin, L. & West, A. (2016) 'Careers in the outdoors', in Humberstone, B., Prince, H. & Henderson, K. (eds) *Routledge International Handbook of Outdoor Studies*. London: Routledge.

Archard, J. (2015) 'The Impact of Regular Forest School Sessions on Young Teenagers' Wellbeing'. Torpoint: Silvanus Trust. Available at https://good fromwoods.wordpress.com/case-studies/

Aspinall, P., Mavros, P., Coyne, R. & Roe, J. (2013) 'The urban brain: analysing outdoor physical activity with mobile EEG', *British Journal of Sports Medicine*, 49(4): 272–6.

Aubrey, K. & Riley, A. (2015) *Understanding and Using Educational Theories*. London: Sage.

Barnardos (2008) 'Outcomes-Focused Children's Services', *ChildLinks*, 2.

Barnardos (2011) 'Children's Risky Play', *ChildLinks*, 3.

Barnes, S. (2007) *How to be Wild*. London: Short Books.

Beames, S. & Brown, M. (2016) *Adventurous Learning: a Pedagogy for a Changing World*. London: Routledge.

Berntsen, S., Mowinckel, P., Carlsen, K., Lødrup Carlsen, K., Pollestad Kolsgaard, M., Joner, G. & Anderssen, S. (2010) 'Obese children playing towards an active lifestyle', *International Journal of Pediatric Obesity*, 5(1): 64–71.

Bird, W. (2007) 'Natural Thinking: Investigating the Links between the Natural Environment, Biodiversity and Mental Health'. Report for the RSPB. Available at www.rspb.org.uk/Images/naturalthinking_tcm9-161856.pdf

Bligh, C., Chambers, S., Davison, C., Lloyd, I., Musgrave, J., O'Sullivan, J. & Waltham, S. (2013) *Well-being in the Early Years*. Northwich: Critical Publishing.

Boodhna, G. (2013) 'Children's Body Mass Index, Overweight and Obesity'. *The Health Survey for England 2013*. Available at www.hscic.gov.uk/catalogue/PUB16076/HSE2013-Ch11-Child-BMI.pdf

Borradaile, L. (2006) *Forest School Scotland: An Evaluation*. Edinburgh: Forestry Commission Scotland.

Box, A. (2015) 'Forest School Case Study', paper presented to Natural Health Service Conference, Addenbrooke's Hospital, July. Available at http://ecosys temsknowledge.net/sites/default/files/wp-content/uploads/2015/150708_ Cambridge/Allison%20Box_A%20Greenspace%20and%20Health%20Case %20Study_Forest%20Schools.pdf

Bratton, C., Crossey, U., Crosby, D. & McKeown, W. (2009) 'Learning Outdoors in the Early Years'. Belfast: Early Years Interboard Panel. Available at http://ccea.org.uk/sites/default/files/docs/curriculum/area_of_ learning/fs_learning_outdoors_resource_book.pdf

Bruce, T. (2012) *Early Childhood Practice: Froebel Today*. London: Sage.

Bryson, B. (1997) *A Walk in the Woods*. London: Transworld Publishers.

Burls, A. (2007) 'People and green spaces: promoting public health and mental well-being through ecotherapy', *Journal of Public Mental Health*, 6(3): 24–38.

Burrows, K. (2011) 'Autism, art and nature as relational aspects of forest school', in Knight, S. (ed.) *Forest School for All*. London: Sage

Burrows, K. (2012) 'Art in woodland: creating a holding environment for students with autism', in Pryor, A., Carpenter, C., Norton, C. & Kirchner, J. (eds) *Emerging Insights: Proceedings of the 5th Adventure Therapy Conference 2009*. Prague: European Science and Art Publishing.

Cartwright, I. (2012) 'Informal education in compulsory schooling in the UK: humanising moments, utopian spaces?', in Kraftl, P., Horton, J. & Tucker, F. (eds) *Critical Geographies of Childhood and Youth: Policy and Practice*. Bristol: The Policy Press.

Casey, E. (2001) 'Between geography and philosophy: what does it mean to be in the place-world?', *Annals of the Association of American Geographers*, 91(4): 683–93.

Centre for Early Childhood Development & Education (2006) *Síolta: The National Quality Framework for Early Childhood Education – Infant Classes User Manual*. Dublin: Centre for Early Childhood Development & Education.

Centre for Mental Health & UCL Institute of Education (2015) *Children of the New Century: Mental Health Findings from the Millennium Cohort Study*. London: Centre for Mental Health.

Choat, I. (2016) 'Playing Away: Would You Take Your Kids out of School?'. Available at www.theguardian.com/travel/2016/jan/29/is-world-schooling-kids-selfish-family-travel-edventures

Christie, B., Beames, S., Higgins, P., Nicol, R. & Ross, H. (2014) 'Outdoor learning provision in Scottish Schools', *Scottish Educational Review*, 46(1): 48–64.

Christie, B., Higgins, P. & Nicol, R. (2016) 'Curricular outdoor learning in Scotland', in Humberstone, B., Prince, H. & Henderson, K. (eds) *Routledge International Handbook of Outdoor Studies*. London: Routledge.

Claxton, G. (2005) *Building Learning Power*. Bristol: The Learning Organisation (TLO).

Claxton, G., Chambers, M., Powell, G. & Lucas, B. (2011) *The Learning Powered School: Pioneering 21st Century Education*. Bristol: TLO.

Cole, M. (2012) 'Racism and education: from empire to ConDem', in Cole, M. (ed.) *Education, Equality and Human Rights*. London: Routledge.

Committee on the Rights of the Child (1995) 'Concluding observations of the Committee on the Rights of the Child: United Kingdom of Great Britain and Northern Ireland', in *The Convention on the Rights of the Child*. London: United Nations Children's Emergency Fund (UNICEF).

Cooke, J. (2016) *The Treeclimber's Guide to London*. London: Harper Collins.

Council for the Curriculum, Examinations and Assessment (2007) *The Northern Ireland Curriculum: Primary*. Belfast: Council for the Curriculum, Examinations and Assessment.

Council for the Curriculum, Examinations and Assessment (2014) *The Curricular Guidance for Pre-School Education*. Belfast: Council for the Curriculum, Examinations and Assessment.

Cree, J. (2011) 'Maintaining the forest school ethos while working with 14–19-year-old boys', in Knight, S. (ed.) *Forest School for All*. London: Sage.

Cree, J. & Gersie, A. (2014) 'Storytelling in the woods', in Gersie, A., Nanson, A. & Schieffelin, E. (eds) *Storytelling for a Greener World*. Stroud: Hawthorn Press.

Cree, J. & McCree, M. (2014) 'History of Forest School'. Available at www.forestschoolassociation.org/history-of-forest-school/

Cunningham, H. (2006) *The Invention of Childhood*. London: BBC Books.

Curriculum Review Group, The (2004) *A Curriculum for Excellence*. Edinburgh: Scottish Executive.

Cuyler, M. & Mathieu, J. (2014) *We're Going on a Lion Hunt*. Las Vegas, NV: Amazon Publishing.

Davis, B. & Waite, S. (2005) *Forest Schools: An Evaluation of the Opportunities and Challenges in Early Years – Final Report January 2005*. Plymouth: Plymouth University.

Davis, J. (ed.) (2015) *Young Children and the Environment*. Port Melbourne: Cambridge University Press.

Deakin, R. (2008) *Wildwood: A Journey through Trees*. London: Penguin.

Dept for Children, Schools and Families (DCSF) (2008) *Practice Guidance for the Early Years Foundation Stage*. London: DCSF.

Dept for Education (DfE) (2013) 'The National Curriculum in England: Key Stages 1 and 2 Framework Document DFE-00178-2013'. London: DfE. Available at www.gov.uk/government/uploads/system/uploads/attachment_data/file/425601/PRIMARY_national_curriculum.pdf

DfE (2014a) 'Statutory Framework for the Early Years Foundation Stage', Ref. No. DFE-00337-2014. London: English Government. Available at www.gov.uk/government/publications/early-years-foundation-stage-framework--2

DfE (2014b) 'Evidence Check Memorandum: School Starting Age'. London: English Government. Available at www.parliament.uk/documents/commons-committees/Education/evidence-check-forum/School-starting-age.pdf

DfE (2015) 'Statistical First Release: Special Educational Needs in England – January 2015'. Available at www.gov.uk/government/uploads/system/uploads/attachment_data/file/447917/SFR25-2015_Text.pdf

DfE and Dept of Health (DoH) (2015) 'Special Educational Needs and Disability Code of Practice: 0 to 25 Years'. Available at www.gov.uk/government/uploads/system/uploads/attachment_data/file/398815/SEND_Code_of_Practice_January_2015.pdf

Dept for Education and Skills (DFES) (2014) *Further Steps Outdoors: Guidance*. Cardiff: Welsh Government.

DFES (2015) *Curriculum for Wales: Foundation Phase Framework*. Cardiff: Welsh Government. Available at http://learning.gov.wales/resources/browse-all/foundation-phase-framework/?lang=en

Dept of Education, Northern Ireland (DENI) (2015) 'Statistical Bulletin 8/2015: Annual Enrolments at Grant-aided Schools in Northern Ireland 2015/16'. Belfast: Dept of Education. Available at www.deni.gov.uk/sites/default/file/spublications/de/statistical-bulletin-annual-enrolments-at-grant-aided-schools-in-Northern-Ireland-2015-16-basic-provisional-statistics.pdf

Dighton, R. (2008) *An Ethical Basis for Good Practice in Play Therapy*. Weybridge: British Association of Play Therapists.

Donaldson, G. (2015) *Successful Futures: Independent Review of Curriculum and Assessment Arrangements in Wales*. Cardiff: Welsh Government. Available at http://gov.wales/docs/dcells/publications/150317-successful-futures-en.pdf

Dorling, D. (2016) 'England's schools make us the extremists of Europe', *The Guardian* (Education section), 23 February. Available at www.theguardian.com/education/2016/feb/23/england-schools-extremists-europe-tests-excludes-elitism

Education Scotland (2010) *Curriculum for Excellence through Outdoor Learning*. Glasgow: Learning and Teaching Scotland. Available at www.educationscotland.gov.uk/learningandteaching/approaches/outdoorlearning/about/cfethroughoutdoorlearning.asp

Education Scotland (2012) *Curriculum for Excellence through Outdoor Learning and the Curriculum for Excellence: Assessing Progress and Achievement in the 3–15 Broad General Education*. Glasgow: Learning and Teaching Scotland. Available at www.educationscotland.gov.uk/Images/CfEbriefing2_tcm4-730387.pdf

Eernstman, N. & Wals, N. (2013) 'Locative meaning-making: an arts-based approach to learning for sustainable development', *Sustainability*, 5: 1645–60.

Else, P. (2009) *The Value of Play*. London: Continuum.

European Commission/EACEA/Eurydice (2015) *Compulsory Education in Europe 2015/16: Eurydice Facts and Figures*. Luxembourg: Publications Office of the European Union. Available at http://bookshop.europa.eu/is-bin/INTERSHOP.enfinity/WFS/EU-Bookshop-Site/en_GB/-/EUR/ViewPublication-Start?PublicationKey=ECAP15002

Forest School Association (FSA) (2011) 'Full Principles and Criteria for Good Practice'. Available at www.forestschoolassociation.org/full-principles-and-criteria-for-good-practice/

FSA (2015a) 'GB Forest School Trainers Network and the FSA'. Available at www.forestschoolassociation.org/gb-forest-school-trainers-network-and-the-fsa/

FSA (2015b) 'Fire Lighting and Management'. Available at www.forestschool association.org/wiki/practical-skills/fire-lighting-and-management-home-page-do-not-alter/

FSA (2016a) 'Qualified Forest School Practitioner Database'. Available at www.forestschoolassociation.org/qualified-forest-school-practitioner-database/

FSA (2016b) 'What is Forest School?'. Available at www.forestschoolassocia tion.org/what-is-forest-school/

Forestry Commission Scotland (FCS) (2013) *The Role of Scotland's National Forest Estate and Strategic Directions*. Edinburgh: FCS.

General Teaching Council (GTC) for Scotland (2014) *Professional Update Guidance Notes*. Edinburgh: GTC Scotland.

Gill, T. (2007) *No Fear: Growing Up in a Risk Averse Society*. London: Caloustie Gulbenkian Foundation.

Gill, T. (2014) 'The benefits of children's engagement with nature: a systematic literature review', *Children, Youth and Environments*, 24(2): 10–34.

Goleman, D. (1996) *Emotional Intelligence*. London: Bloomsbury Publishing.

Goulson, D. (2014) *A Buzz in the Meadow*. London: Vintage Books.

Gray, D.S. (2012) 'Walking in the mindfield', *International Journal of Holistic Education*, 1(1): 1–8.

Greenaway, R. & Knapp, C. (2016) 'Reviewing and reflection: connecting people top experiences', in Humberstone, B., Prince, H. & Henderson, K. (eds) *Routledge International Handbook of Outdoor Studies*. London: Routledge.

Grossmann, K. & Grossmann, K. (2007) 'The impact of attachment to mother and father at an early age on children's psychosocial development through young adulthood', in *Encyclopedia on Early Childhood Development*. Montreal: Centre of Excellence for Early Childhood Development. Available at www.child-encyclopedia.com/Pages/PDF/GrossmannANGxp_rev.pdf

Gurholt, K. (2016) 'Friluftsliv: nature-friendly adventures for all', in Humberstone, B., Prince, H. & Henderson, K. (eds) *Routledge International Handbook of Outdoor Studies*. London: Routledge.

Harris, F. (2015) 'The nature of learning at forest school: practitioners' perspectives', *Education 3–13*. E-pub ahead of print, 11 September.

Health and Safety Executive (HSE) (2012) 'Children's Play and Leisure: Promoting a Balanced Approach'. Available at www.hse.gov.uk/entertainment/childs-play-statement.htm

Hilary, B. (2009) *Childhood and Nature: A Survey on Changing Relationships with Nature across Generations*. London: Natural England.

Hopkins, F. (2011) 'Removing barriers: getting children with physical challenges into the woods', in Knight, S. (ed.) *Forest School for All*. London: Sage.

Horning, A. (2011) 'Using forest school to make the transition to high school', in Knight, S. (ed.) *Forest School for All*. London: Sage.

Horseman, L. & Scott, J. (2010) 'Forest Schools Bradford West'. Available at http://kindlingplayandtraining.co.uk/forest-schools/

Hughes, F. (2007) *Pentre Forest School: An Evaluation of a Forest School Project*. Ruthin: Forestry Commission Wales.

Hughes, B. (2012) *Evolutionary Playwork*. Abingdon: Routledge.

Hughes, F. & Jenner, L. (2006) *Pentre Forest School: An Evaluation of a Forest School Project*. Ruthin: Forestry Commission Wales.

Jackson, S. & Forbes, R. (2015) *People under Three: Play, Work and Learning in a Childcare Setting*. Abingdon: Routledge.

Jouret, B., Ahluwalia, N., Cristini, C., Dupuy, M., Nègre-Pages, L., Grandjean, H. & Tauber, M. (2007) 'Factors associated with overweight in preschool-age children in southwestern France', *American Journal of Clinical Nutrition*, 85: 1643–9.

Jung, C.G. (1967) *Memories, Dreams, Reflections*. London: Fontana.

Kaplan, R. & Kaplan, S. (1995) *The Experience of Nature: A Psychological Perspective*. New York: Cambridge University Press.

Kardan, O., Gozdyra, P., Misic, B., Moola, F., Palmer, L., Paus, T. & Berman, M. (2015) 'Neighborhood greenspace and health in a large urban centre', *Scientific Reports 5*, Article no. 11610.

Kellert, S. & Wilson, E.O. (eds) (1993) *The Biophilia Hypothesis*. Washington, DC: Island Press.

Knight, S. (2013) *Forest School and Outdoor Play in the Early Years*. London: Sage.

Knight, S. (2015) 'Working with forest schools', in Maynard, T. & Waters, J. (eds) *Exploring Outdoor Play in the Early Years*. Maidenhead: Open University Press.

Knight, S. (2016a) ' Forest school in the United Kingdom', in Humberstone, B., Prince, H. & Henderson, K. (eds) *Routledge International Handbook of Outdoor Studies*. London: Routledge.

Knight, S. (2016b) 'Forest school: a model for learning holistically and out-doors', in Lees, H.E. & Noddings, N. (eds) *The Palgrave International Handbook of Alternative Education*. London: Palgrave Macmillan.

Knight, S. (2016c) 'Forest School for the early years in England', in Waller, T. (ed.) *Sage Handbook of Outdoor Play and Learning*. London: Sage.

Knight, S. (2016d) 'Forest school: opportunities for creative and spiritual growth', in Pickering, S. (ed.) *Teaching Outdoors Creatively*. London: Routledge.

Kohn, A. (2006) *Beyond Discipline: From Compliance to Community*. Alexandria, VA: ASCD.

Lamb, C. (2011) 'Forest school: a whole school approach', in Knight, S. (ed.) *Forest School for All*. London: Sage.

Leach, J. (2013) 'Happiness Grows on Trees: How Woodlands Boost our Wellbeing'. Available at www.woodlands.co.uk/Woodlands.co.uk-Happi nessGrowsOnTrees-Feb13.pdf

Learning and Teaching Scotland (2007) *A Curriculum for Excellence: Building the Curriculum 2 – Active Learning in the Early Years*. Edinburgh: Scottish Qualifications Authority.

Leather, M. (2012) 'Seeing the Wood from the Trees: Constructionism and Constructivism for Outdoor and Experiential Education'. Edinburgh: University of Edinburgh. Available at http://oeandphilosophy2012.newhar bour.co.uk/wp-content/uploads/2012/04/Mark-Leather.pdf

Lindon, J. (2003) *Too Safe for their Own Good?* London: National Children's Bureau.

Louv, R. (2009) *Last Child in the Woods: Saving our Children from Nature-Deficit Disorder*. London: Atlantic.

Lucas, B., Claxton, G. & Spencer, E. (2013) *Expansive Education*. Maidenhead: Open University Press.

Luff, P. & Knight, S. (2014) 'Report on Workshop on the Role of Forest Schools in Early Childhood Education for Sustainability'. Available at www.forestschoolassociation.org/outputs-from-forest-school-association-national-conference-2014-danbury-essex/

Male, T. & Palaiologou, I. (2016) 'Historical developments in policy for early years education and care', in Palaiologou, I. (ed.) *The Early Years Foundation Stage*. London: Sage.

Martin, J. (2012) 'Gender and education: continuity and difference', in Cole, M. (ed.) *Education, Equality and Human Rights*. London: Routledge.

Milchem, K. (2011) 'Breaking through concrete: the emergence of forest school in London', in Knight, S. (ed.) *Forest School for All*. London: Sage.

Mind (2016) 'Mental Health Taskforce Report: The Five Year Forward View for Mental Health'. Available at www.crisiscareconcordat.org.uk/wp-content/uploads/2016/02/Mental-Health-Taskforce-FYFV-final-1.pdf

Mitten, D. (2009) 'The healing power of nature: the need for nature for human health, development, and wellbeing', paper presented at Ibsen: Friluftsliv Jubilee Conference, Levanger, Norway, 14–19 September. Available at http://norwegianjournaloffriluftsliv.com/doc/122010.pdf

Moore, R. (1993) *Plants for Play*. Berkeley, CA: MIG Communications.

Moore, R. (2015) *Nature Play and Learning Places*. Raleigh, NC: Natural Learning Initiative; and Reston, VA: National Wildlife Federation. Available at https://natureplayandlearningplaces.org/

Nanson, A. (2014) 'Jumping the gap of desire: telling stories from ecological history about species extinctions to evoke an empathetic and questioning response', in Gersie, A., Nanson, A. & Schieffelin, E. (eds) *Storytelling for a Greener World: Environment, Community and Story-based Learning*. Stroud: Hawthorn Press.

National Council for Curriculum and Assessment (1999) *Primary School Curriculum: Introduction*. Dublin: Department of Education and Science. Available at www.ncca.ie/en/Curriculum_and_Assessment/Early_Child hood_and_Primary_Education/Primary-Education/Primary_School_ Curriculum/

National Council for Curriculum and Assessment (2009) *Aistear: The Early Childhood Curriculum Framework – Guidelines for Good Practice*. Dublin: Department of Education and Science.

Natural Resources Wales (2015) *A Guide to Forest School in Wales*. Cardiff: Natural Resources Wales.

Nilsson, K., Sangster, M. & Konijnendijk, C. (2011) 'Forests, trees and human health and wellbeing: introduction', in Nilsson, K., Sangster, M. & Konijnendijk, C. (eds) *Forests, Trees and Human Health and Well-being*. Dordrecht: Springer.

O'Brien, L. (2009) 'Learning outdoors: the forest school approach', *Education 3–13*, 37(1): 45–60.

O'Brien, L. & Murray, R. (2007) 'Forest school and its impacts on young children: case studies in Britain', *Urban Forestry & Urban Greening*, 6: 249–65.

Ofsted (2012) *Using a Forest Environment for Pre-school Children*. London: Ofsted.

Öhman, J. and Sandell, K. (2016) 'Environmental concerns and outdoor studies: nature as fosterer', in Humberstone, B., Prince, H. & Henderson, K. (eds) *Routledge International Handbook of Outdoor Studies*. London: Routledge.

Osgood, J. (2008) 'Professionalism and performativity: the feminist challenge facing early years practitioners', in Wood, E. (ed.) *The Routledge Reader in Early Childhood Education*. London: Routledge.

Outdoor and Woodland Learning (OWL) Scotland (2014) 'FS Practitioner Location Map'. Available at http://owlscotland.org/images/uploads/resources/files/FS_Practitioners_Location_Map_vNov2014.pdf

OWL Outdoor and Woodland Learning Scotland (2015) 'Forest School Case Studies'. Available at http://owlscotland.org/site/search/89bb7c6a6e49cdc390872faeb13be92c/

Oxfordshire Children's Trust (2015) 'Oxfordshire Children and Young People's Plan'. Oxford: Oxfordshire County Council. Available at www.oxfordshire.gov.uk/cms/sites/default/files/folders/documents/childreneducationandfamilies/workingwithchildren/ChildrenYoung_People_Plan_full.pdf

Palmer, S. (2016) *Upstart: The Case for Raising the School Starting Age and Providing what the Under-sevens Really Need*. Edinburgh: Floris Books.

Partridge, L. & Taylor, W. (2011) 'Forest school for families', in Knight, S. (ed.) *Forest School for All*. London: Sage.

Pavey, B. (2006) 'The Forest School and Inclusion: A Project Evaluation'. Available at www.leeds.ac.uk/educol/documents/161165.htm

Pramling Samuelsson, I. & Kaga, Y. (2010) 'Early childhood education to transform cultures for sustainability', in *State of the World 2010: Transforming Cultures from Consumerism to Sustainability*, 27th edn. London/New York: Worldwatch Institute.

Rees, G., Andresen, S. & Bradshaw, J. (eds) (2016) *Children's Views on their Lives and Well-being in 16 Countries: A Report on the Children's Worlds Survey of Children Aged Eight Years Old, 2013–15*. York: Children's Worlds Project (ISCWeB).

Ridgers, N. & Sayers, J. (2010) *Natural Play in the Forest: Forest School Evaluation*. London: Natural England.

Rieser, R. (2012a) 'Inclusive education', in Cole, M. (ed.) *Education, Equality and Human Rights*. London: Routledge.

Rieser, R. (2012b) 'The Struggle for Inclusion: The Growth of a Movement'. Available at http://worldofinclusion.com/struggle-for-inclusion/

Roe, J., Aspinall, P. & Ward Thompson, C. (2008) *Forest School: Evidence for Restorative Health Benefits in Young People*. Edinburgh: Forestry Commission Scotland.

Roe, J.J., Thompson, C.W., Aspinall, P.A., Brewer, M.J., Duff, E.I., Miller, D., et al. (2013) 'Green space and stress: evidence from cortisol measures in deprived urban communities', *International Journal of Environmental Research and Public Health*, 10(9): 4086–103.

Sallis, J.F. & Owen, N. (2002) 'Ecological models of health behavior', in Glanz, K., Rimer, B. & Lewis, F. (eds) *Health Behavior and Health Education*, 3rd edn. San Francisco, CA: John Wiley & Sons.

Santostefano, S. (2004) *Child Therapy and the Great Outdoors*. London: Analytical Press.

Savery, A., Cain, T., Garner, J., Jones, T., Kynaston, E., Mould, K., et al. (2016) 'Does engagement in forest school influence perceptions of risk?', *Education 3–13*, 18 February. Available at www.tandfonline.com/doi/abs/10.1080/03004279.2016.1140799

Schofield, J. & Danks, F. (2009) *Go Wild: 101 Things to Do Outdoors Before You Grow Up*. London: Frances Lincoln.

Scottish Government (2015) 'Scottish Index of Multiple Deprivation'. Available at www.gov.scot/Topics/Statistics/SIMD

Scout Association (2013) 'Fire Lighting Essentials'. Available at www.scout activitycentres.org.uk/wp-content/uploads/2014/01/fireLighting-Facts heet.pdf

Selhub, E. & Logan, A. (2014) *Your Brain on Nature*. Toronto: John Wiley & Sons.

Sempik, J., Hine, R. & Wilcox, D. (2010) 'Green Care: A Conceptual Framework – A Report of the Working Group on the Health Benefits of Green Care'. COST Action 866, Green Care in Agriculture. Loughborough: Centre for Child and Family Research, Loughborough University.

Shier, H. (2001) 'Pathways to participation: openings, opportunities and obligations', *Children & Society*, 15: 107–17.

Smith, J. (2015) *Making Sense of Ecotherapy*. London: Mind.

Sunderland, M. (2012) 'The Science of Parenting', notes from lecture given at the Baby Friendly Initiative Conference 2012. Available at http://unicef.org.uk/Documents/Baby_Friendly/Conference/Presentations/2012/Parenting_Margot_Sunderland_BFI_Conf_2012.pdf

Sunderland, M. (2013) 'Winning Hearts and Minds in Forest School', notes from lecture given at the Forest School Association National Conference 2013, Derwent Hill OEC. Available at www.forestschoolassociation.org/post-conference-2013-resources/

Thriftwood School (2015) 'Outdoor Learning'. Available at www.thriftwood school.com/page/?title=Outdoor+Learning&pid=78

Tudge, C. (2006) *The Secret Life of Trees*. London: Penguin, first published in 2005.

UNICEF UK (2013) 'Report Card 11: The Well-being of Children: How does the UK Score?'. Available at www.unicef.org.uk/rc11

United Nations Enable (2016) 'Convention on the Rights of Persons with Disabilities'. Available at www.un.org/disabilities/default.asp?navid=15&pid=150

Vinning, J., Merrick, M. & Price, E. (2008) 'The distinction between humans and nature: human perceptions of connectedness to nature and elements of the natural and unnatural', *Human Ecology Review*, 15(1): 1–11.

Vision Council, The (2015) *Hindsight is 20/20/20: Protect Your Eyes from Digital Devices – 2015 Digital Eye Strain Report*. Vancouver: The Vision Council. Available at www.thevisioncouncil.org/sites/default/files/VC_DigitalEyeStrain_Report2015.pdf

Warden, C. (2012) *Nature Kindergartens and Forest Schools*. Auchterader: Mindstretchers.

Warden, C. (2015) *Learning with Nature: Embedding Outdoor Practice*. London: Sage.

Waters, P. (2011) 'Trees talk: are you listening? Nature, narrative and children's anthropocentric place-based play', *Children, Youth and Environments*, 21(1): 243–52.

Wattchow, B. & Brown, M. (2011) *A Pedagogy of Place*. Melbourne: Monash University Publishing.

Wicks, R. (2011) 'Forest school and looked after children', in Knight, S. (ed.) *Forest School for All*. London: Sage.

Index

Figures are indicated by page numbers in bold print. The letters '*bib*' after a page number refer to bibliographical information in the 'Further Reading' sections.